A New Dimension in Old Testament Study

A Course Guide to the Study of Selections From the Old Testament for Individuals and Groups

by

Sadie Gregory

San Francisco, Guild for Psychological Studies, 1980

Guild for Psychological Studies
2230 Divisadero Street
San Francisco, California 94115

Table of Contents

Acknowledgements

The specific seminar method and many of the various suggestions found in the "Beyond Discussion" section of the "Introduction" were developed during my work with the Guild for Psychological Studies located in San Francisco, California. This group has been at work for more than forty years developing through experience new emphases and new techniques. It still, today, stands in the forefront of an age of transition, helping many persons find a new sense of value and meaning in the face of the increasing pull of the collective.

Its work is rooted in Henry Burton Sharman's The Records of the Life of Jesus and is amplified by the psychology of C. G. Jung. With this as the basic ground work, texts from many other sources are used as seminar material. These additional texts include Old Testament passages and writings from Teilhard de Chardin, Paul Tillich, Martin Buber, Fritz Kunkel, Nikos Kazantzakis, Charles Williams, J. R. R. Tolkien, and others. World myth and folktale, too, have an important place in Guild seminars.

To the founding leaders of the Guild, Dr. Elizabeth B. Howes, Dr. Sheila Moon, and Miss Luella Sibbald, I want to express my deeply felt appreciation for all I have received through participation in and leadership of Guild seminars and training programs. Also, I express gratitude for their encouragement of this project and for their reading of the manuscript.

To Miss Florence Little, the Guild Librarian, for her encouragement and for her many readings of the manuscript at various stages in its development, I express my sincere thanks.

Lastly, I wish to thank all who have participated in seminars on material from the Old Testament for their rich enthusiastic responses and for frequent requests for Old Testament material. This course is a first response. A second course on Great Themes of the Old Testament *is being planned for the future.*

Sadie Gregory
San Francisco
July, 1980

Introduction

A. WHY STUDY THE OLD TESTAMENT?

Outer space has been one of the great frontiers of our day. Humans have walked upon the surface of the moon and continue to probe farther into galactic and intergalactic distances. If in the long run this is to be a true advance, it must be paralleled by continuing explorations into inner space. A comparable amount of energy and attention must be spent by the equally adventurous in exploring new ways to deal with the untold realities of the inner world. Dr. C. G. Jung ventured far into this field and has contributed a fund of knowledge, experience, clues, and tools for those who would follow him. Much of the violence erupting in the world today is rooted in unconscious factors at work in individual psyches. Hence it behooves us to press forward into the field that Freud and Jung opened up. These unconscious factors need to be drawn into consciousness and dealt with on a personal level.

One excellent source of help in this adventuring into interior space can be the Old Testament. From personal work with it, and from using material from it with groups, I have discovered that much Old Testament material can be a significant help on the inward journey. How can a study of Old Testament material help modern individuals face life in an age of transition? Let me attempt to answer this question.

Among the many demands of the new age is the challenge to frankness and direct confrontation. In Martin Buber's terms an "I-Thou" is essential between an individual and nature, between persons, between an individual and the "Eternal Thou." The validity of the first two depend on their being rooted in the relationship with the "Eternal Thou." Where else in literature can one find so much of the dialogue with God as is to be found in the Old Testament? From the tale of Adam talking to the Lord God in the cool of the evening, through the high peaks in the lives of the major prophets and the book of Job, there is a rich flow of dialogue between individuals and God. To the participants these dialogues were experienced as confrontation with the transcendent aspect of God. Today we might experience such an encounter as a confrontation with the God within, with God active in the factors of the existential moment, or with God transcendent — the "Wholly Other." What is important again in our day is to know that there is a Thou immeasurably greater than the personal I and that relationship with that Other is possible and essential for health and fulfillment. A living acquaintance with the great Yahweh-person encounters of the Old Testament can awaken one's heart to the possibility of deeper personal encounters with the Other.

In the Old Testament one meets with a wide variety of aspects of the image of God. Various aspects of the many-faceted image can be found in the great cosmic myths, the hero stories, the history, the laws, the teachings, and the lives of the prophets. The many-faceted image is revealed in different types of Old Testament material and in writings from many different historical eras. Such qualities as graciousness and petulance, decisiveness and indecision, justice and injustice, wrath and compassion, love and hatred are manifested. No image of God can begin to encompass the Reality. That can never be known. To try to limit that image largely to light and perfection, as much of Christianity has done, is to narrow one's ability to encompass the experience of God. To confront honestly the many aspects of God as revealed in the Old Testament is to broaden one's knowledge of life itself, to grow in one's experience of the God behind all the images and thus to be able to come into a fuller relationship with the Other.

Any deep understanding of Jesus necessitates some knowledge of the Old Testament. Jesus was rooted and grounded in it, and if we want to come to grips with his meaning today, we must know something of the religious roots that nourished his development.

Whether Jew or Christian, if we want to become more whole persons, we need to rediscover the neglected Judaic images in our own unconscious. Only thus can we begin to relate to them and to integrate them into our conscious being.

The Old Testament contains much potent material from deep levels within the human psyche. In it there are cosmic myths, folktales, and hero stories; sacred rites, ancient laws, a book of praise, and short stories, as well as the history of a people and its developing relationship with God. Depth psychology has brought to our attention the value of such material as providing symbolic clues to self understanding. Myths arise from an inner reality and speak by way of symbols to one who has ears to hear, a mind open to different aspects of truth, and a heart seeking answers to life's meaning. As Frances Wickes has stated in The Inner World of Choice:

> As psychic history, myth tells of man's search for understanding of the mysteries of his own life and his experience of the world in which he finds himself. Such narrative has been handed down to us not because of its historical accuracy but because of its numinous dynamic quality. It is true in a non-factual living way that brings man nearer to the meaning of his life.

The use of selected Old Testament material has proved again and again its effectiveness in helping individuals to richer living. The vitality of the discussion, the results from the related use of the art media, movement, and ritual have all revealed the dynamic nature of the chosen material. Many individuals who have participated in such seminars consistently report the continuing help received from such study.

B. THE NEW DIMENSION

For some of us our knowledge of the Old Testament began with stories told in Church School classes or read from one of many collections of Old Testament tales retold for children. These stories are often (though unfortunately not always) well told and well used in Church Schools. Knowing some of the stories and enjoying them is what I would call the first level of Old Testament appreciation. This is an important level and it is sad to realize how little, if at all, the material is used nowadays in the public schools. With the current decrease in Church School attendance more and more children are growing into adulthood without any knowledge of the rich resources for living that are to be found in the Old Testament.

A second level of knowledge comes when one has the opportunity to study the history of Biblical times and the growth of Biblical literature. My first course in Old Testament, taken with a Student Christian Movement graduate study group in Manitoba, was full of excitement and delight for me and came at a time when I was just beginning to teach the Religious Knowledge courses at what was then Riverbend School for Girls in Winnipeg, Manitoba. To study Old Testament and to discover something of the overall development of the literature was a great satisfaction. More than a decade later I was able to pursue my interest in Old Testament under Dr. James Muilenburg at Union Theological Seminary in New York City. Again the excitement of study with an outstanding Old Testament teacher filled with enthusiasm for his subject added to my conceptual knowledge and deepened my enthusiasm for working in the area of the Old Testament.

The third dimension of my personal experience with the Old Testament came when I discovered the Guild for Psychological Studies. This group includes the depth psychological approach in all its seminar discussions. With this approach to the Old Testament material a whole new dimension is brought into focus, one that can help individuals to reach new depths in the psyche.

To help clarify the approach used in A New Dimension in Old Testament Study, I shall attempt to give definitions of a few of the basic terms used in the psychology of Dr. C. G. Jung. His ideas were in a state of continual and rich evolution throughout his lifetime. Hence it follows that what is said in earlier works is modified by later discoveries. Granted, these definitions will give but a brief and, of necessity, partial glance into a vast field that in itself needs much study and personal experience. However, the few terms used are now more or less common parlance, having moved into the current vocabulary. An acceptance of the validity of the unconscious as a dynamic force in daily life makes available a very different level from which to answer the questions asked.

The word "ego," as used by Jung, is the center of the conscious personality. It is the chooser and that which can relate to the unconscous as it comes into consciousness. Unless a person exercises an ego-relationship to unconscious material there can be a swamping by the flood of images that may arise in given situations. Hence the ego is of central importance. However it is not the center of the total personality. In fact, consciousness is but a part of the total person and doesn't begin to play the dominant role modern rational humans have credited to it.

Out of his experience Jung came to differentiate between the "personal unconscious" and the "collective unconscious." The personal unconscious contains all that the individual has repressed or suppressed — such as things feared, unfaced traumas, inklings of unknown strengths. "Below" this level of the personal unconscious lies the collective unconscious. This is a universal substratum of patterned responses coming from the primitive beginnings of life. "It is a potentiality handed down from primordial times" giving "inborn possibilities of ideas." (C. G. Jung, Collected Works, 15, pg. 80-81)

At the heart of Jung's use of the term "psyche" lies the fact that it consists of two parts — the conscious and the unconscious. The conflict in each individual between conscious and unconscious is one evidence of the polaristic nature of the psyche. Jung states that he is "of the opinion that the psyche is the most tremendous fact of human life" and that it is "the mother of all things because before they appear in fact they are present in the psyche."

The "archetypes" are inherited patterns of behavior "in" the collective unconscious. Different archetypes are activated at different stages of the individual journey. Among the more familiar archetypes are those of the mother, the father, the child, and the savior. The "Self" is a central archetype and perhaps the most difficult to define. The Self is infinitely larger than the ego, for while the ego is the center of the conscious personality, the Self is the center of the total personality. In the Self lie all the opposites and from it comes that which pushes the individual toward growth and wholeness.

The "shadow" lies mostly "in" the personal unconscious and consists of the negative qualities which one does not wish to acknowledge and the positive qualities for which one does not wish to take responsibility. These hidden qualities, when not incorporated into personal development, are projected onto other people or things. One important task en route to individuation is to draw back the projections that have been made. In themselves projections are not wrong but can be helpful means to discovering facts about oneself. The danger comes when an individual attempts to live with the projection indefinitely and to avoid the development of the personal life.

"Individuation" is the goal sought of work in bringing the conscious and unconscious aspects of the psyche into a new type of relationship. No wholeness can result if either side is neglected. The work of trying to bring these two sides into some sort of relationship causes the arousal of certain symbols in the *psyche. Within the symbol can lie the healing power that makes it possible for the individual to move forward into the next step on the way.*

It is from the recognition of the power the unconscious has in our daily lives and the acknowledgement that the rational is not the sole control of our doings that the questions asked can be grappled with on a new level.

C. ORGANIZATION OF THE COURSE.

There are twelve studies in A New Dimension in Old Testament Study. *The first seven use material about individuals. In some of the earlier studies much of the material related about them is based on oral tradition. In the latter ones more of the material is historical. Studies VIII-X deal with the great cosmic myths found in the early chapters of Genesis. Study XI is based on the two short stories — Ruth and Jonah — while study XII works with three Psalms from the Book of Psalms. Because of the major place the Book of Psalms has had through the centuries, it seemed to me important to include a study dealing with material from the Psalms to illustrate that that type of poetic material can also be greatly enriched by the in-depth approach.*

Many of the studies begin with some background material followed by a synopsis of the story where that is felt to be desirable. Each study needs to rest on its roots. Hence the leader will want to spend some time on the historical and literary background of the texts to be used. Not much of such material will need to come into the session itself but the leader will want to be able to handle questions as they arise or, at least, know where the answer may be found.

One aspect of the background material will need to be brought to the attention of the group as a whole, namely, the fact that the textual material chosen has come from many different sources and from many different centuries. Some of the material comes from before the monarchy was established in 1021 B.C. Much of this material is very ancient and has come down through a long period of oral tradition. Some of the material comes from the time of the monarchy when written records were first established, and some comes from the Exile and later. (For an excellent example of the different types of writing from vastly different eras read Genesis 1-2:4a and Genesis 2:4b-3:24.)

While the material must indeed rest on its roots in history, the leader needs to be constantly aware of the aim of the course which is that each participant may have a stirring confrontation with the selected material. A study of a body of facts about an event can well leave life unchanged; an inner confrontation with the core of the story can bring about a rebirth of attitude and action.

Note that first of all the questions are divided into two parts — A and B. The A questions relate to the facts of the material and are used to clarify the meaning of the passage as it stands. While these questions need normally only a minimum amount of time they are essential because lack of clarity on detail can prove troublesome at later stages of the discussion. The story needs to be dealt with exactly as it is told. Even the "uncomfortable" parts of a tale need to be dealt with and not ignored or re-written!

In the B questions lies the heart of the study. These questions have to do with the symbolic and personal meanings as they arise out of the material. Here there is rarely a question that has but one "right" answer. Each participant answers what seems to be the purport of the questions as that person feels it. The questions include a wide variety such as the following: How might a person try to remain in the Garden of Eden? How have you experienced the Cain in you who could commit murder? How do you feel about Jacob's deception of Esau? How can one get in touch with the Moses within who can free from bondage? This type of question is relevant because the material chosen has its roots deep in the Jewish and the Christian psyche. As the group members grow in the their ability to grapple with this kind of question, new insights come and the level of the group discussion deepens.

The leader will find it important to plan the questions to be used ahead of the session. Not all of the questions can or should be used. The risk in suggesting specific questions is that they may be followed in order and used without considering enough the nature and needs of the given group. It is important, too, to get a variety of answers to any given question. Since the B questions are personal, the answers may have as many different shades of meaning as there are people in the group.

Most of the studies will require two or three two-hour sessions. The leader will find it necessary to keep the discussion moving at a creative pace. Too much pressure to keep moving, or a too leisurely "sauntering" through the material can be equally harmful to fruitful discussion.

D. USING THE TEXT*

A New Dimension in Old Testament Study will be found equally useful for the individual seeking in solitude, for two or three seeking together, or for larger groups. Questions are worded and study units planned so that untrained as well as trained leaders may use them with groups.

For the Individual: Approach each Study and its material, both text, and questions, with the greatest possible openness

---

*This section is taken from The Study Guide for The Choice Is Always Ours with the permission of The Guild for Psychological Studies which has the copyright and Dr. Sheila Moon, the author of the section. There are a few word changes to make the statements refer to the current text.

of mind and heart. One's preconceptions are among the worst enemies of new insights. Continually ask: "What is here for me?" and "What does it mean?" rather than too quickly looking to discover what you already think or hope to find. Open yourself to each text before you even read the questions for that selection. Try to find what it says that helps you toward a deepened understanding of Life. If a symbol has been used try to feel into what it means to you. After you have done all of this, turn to the questions for that selection letting biases and blindnesses be corrected by honest answers.

Much will be added to insight if the answers are written out rather than just "kept in your head." Also it can be very helpful to note for further reference those selections which are particularly meaningful to you and those questions which you feel are still unanswered.

For the Group Member: Much of what is said above is relevant for anyone working as a group member, because group members in this sort of seeking are oriented first of all to their own individual needs. There are, however, certain added factors that enter in when one chooses to seek with a group, whether the group is two or twenty.

A group engaged in this kind of common search (as contrasted, for example, with labor-management groups, policy-making groups, etc.) is not aiming for consensus. No decision is at stake. Except for the general desire to explore the meaning of Life, and the general need for honesty and openness, the search together is an individual task. Yet, a few things are essential to remember, else the group exploration becomes a competition, and is rendered valueless.

Be aware of one another. Listen to one another, not in order to debate, but to learn. Open yourselves to all contributions, being especially attentive to those most unlike your own. We grow by including opposites.

A group is only as fertile as its individual members, each of whom has the responsibility to be willing to risk making genuine responses. You are not being responsible if you hold back because you feel someone else will state your ideas more adequately, or if you usurp too much time.

Opinions about material are irrelevant and a waste of time for everyone. Respond to material and the questions asked and contribute as if to a common container in the center of the group, rather than to the leader. Above all, dare to say from the heart and head what seems real and important to you. Remind yourself that you are not in this search to impress others, or necessarily to help others, but to discover your real self in a new and unique way.

For the Leader: Leadership, whether carried by two people jointly or by one alone, is extremely important in keeping members of the group focused on the particular subject being discussed. The leader is not a lecturer, a dominating director, or someone who "knows all the answers." He is an implementer.

As a leader you need first of all to know what it means to be a member of a group. This helps you to be aware of when the group as a whole needs to move to the next question, (or to stay where it is) and to be sensitive to individual members and their problems of participation.

Secondly, you need to remember that the group method chosen as the one best serving the purpose of illuminating the text is a modified socratic approach in which existential "experiencing" is emphasized over against that of theorizing or intellectualization. It is one in which the individual is helped to make his own discoveries (although the leader needs to be sure the meaning of the text is never distorted to fit an individual opinion.)

Certain aspects of the leader's role can be set forth in such a way, we hope, as to help him become a guide, but never a restrictor. Choose your material and questions for study prior to each meeting, basing your choice on what has been discussed already and on the emphases you believe are needed to progress in understanding the Way. (It is important in this regard to ask for suggestions from the group itself.) As you use the questions in the text be sure you know what they mean. It is not necessary that you know the answers! Do not hesitate to supplement the text questions with your own or to adjust questions and their order according to group responses and to development of the discussion. This means learning to be sensitive to where the group is.

Do not fear silences, those ominous threats to new leaders. Often they are very creative, giving members a chance to feel into the questions asked. Speeches by leaders to fill up silences are poor leadership. If a silence seems uncreative, restate your question, or ask another similar one. If it seems necessary, ask the group to state what is not clear. If this is not productive, move on.

When one or more individuals in a group "overtalk" and tend thus to dominate the group, it is good practice to ask a question which encourages the quiet ones, such as: "And what do the rest of you think?", or "Could we hear from those who haven't spoken?" or some other ingenious words of your own designed to redistribute participation.

Keep the discussion focused on the question, and bring it back if it tends to wander too far afield. Never get caught in approving or disapproving individual answers. If an answer seems quite beside the point, restate the question. Otherwise, honor every contribution no matter how awkward it may seem to you and regardless of whether you agree with it. You are not teaching, but guiding. The criterion of a good discussion is whether each participant has gained new insight.

At the end of each session, it is often helpful to the group to have a brief summary (not an interpretation) of what has been discovered during the discussion. Also, the use of a similar brief summary often vitalizes the start of the succeeding session. These summations are not essential, but can aid discussion if they are succinct and impartial.

A final suggestion: it is not only possible but, in some cases, quite workable to have group members take turns as leaders. Often this is a good solution when a group wishes to work with A New Dimension in Old Testament Study but has no one person to carry full leadership. In this situation each new leader should prepare just as thoroughly as if he/she were the only one involved.

E. BEYOND DISCUSSION.

Beyond discussion many different ways, both verbal and non-verbal, have been found to be effective in helping to deepen the level to which the material reaches. Even where the sessions have to be limited to an hour and a half, it is highly recommended that a minimum of 15-20 minutes be spent in something other than discussion.

1. Writing Answers.

Early in the study and at certain key points throughout give time for written answers to pertinent questions. A sharing of these answers by those willing to do so can prove exceedingly helpful in focussing the work that is being done. Also, everyone gets involved in the writing and some of the less articulate are freed to participate in the discussion of succeeding questions.

2. Using Art Materials

Every study offers opportunities for expression in one of the various art media. Specific suggestions can be made for those who are hesitant to undertake art projects. One helpful suggestion for beginners is the following: Take a colored pastel and with large free movements cover the sheet of paper. Rub over the results with paper toweling or tissues. Then, again, with another color, draw something on the page. Rub over it all a second time with the soft paper. Then, letting the arm move in big free strokes, draw some shape on the paper. When something appears that is satisfying, study it to see what is there.

Theme suggestions can be given early in the course if the leader feels it necessary, but mostly these will suggest themselves very readily. Some expression in color, charcoal, or soft drawing pencil can help objectify the inner happenings. It needs to be clearly understood by all that the aim is to let something speak through from the unconscious. The objective is not to create a work of art but to let something come to birth on paper. Often this sort of freedom is as hard for the artist to experience as for an individual without experience in the art field. However, when one can manage to give freedom to the hand, the unconscious will come through. One technique helpful to all, but particularly so to the professional artist, is to work with the left hand (if the right is used normally) and/or to work with the eyes closed.

To give people a chance to comment on their work can be of inestimable value. It is essential in such a sharing that each speaker talk only of his or her own productions. Because the work is so new, comments from others can influence the individual's reactions to his/her own work. At the outset of such a sharing session, it is well to limit time of responses to two or three minutes depending on the size of the group. The experience can have been so moving that the one sharing can get carried away and monopolize too much time. Having a time limit and sticking to it can help avoid the over-talking problem.

If your quarters are cramped and you feel it would be impossible to experiment in this way, you are wrong! There are but three basic minimum essentials: paper, crayons, and a piece of cardboard to use as a table in one's lap. I have seen exciting things happen for individuals with this limited equipment. Of course, if you have more space available, poster paints, water colors, pastels can add to the possibilities and give people a choice of media. Best of all, if clay is a possibility, offer it. Clay often is the easiest material for beginners to work with, and it is one of the best of the art media to get the controlling mind out of the picture and to let the hands speak from the depths. The use of clay needs more time, more uncarpeted space, and the presence of running water close at hand. However, it is well worth the extra effort if the space is available.

3. Dialoguing.
Another technique to recommend is that the participants dialogue with some character or symbol that has spoken to them from the material. If space is available it is helpful to let people spread out so that they have some sense of being apart from others and are thus freer to enter the experience. (It is advisable to write down such a dialogue, otherwise much of what occurs gets forgotten. With the written account, one can go back later to study what has been said and to work with it.) To dialogue with the inward is difficult for many but worth trying because of the help it can be for those who respond to it. One way to begin such a dialogue is to ask a question of the one with whom the dialogue is to take place. Wait in relaxed silence for the answer. Then proceed to question or comment on the answer you are given. Listen again. Sometimes there is a temptation to manipulate the "discussion" and to give in answer what the ego thinks should be said. When you catch this occurring, relax a moment; then wait. Don't hurry or force your attempts to work with this method. The secret is patience, letting go, letting come. This technique can become increasingly useful with practice and is a very helpful tool in the work of self discovery.

The results of this type of dialogue are often too personal to be shared. However, it can be helpful to those having difficulty with the method to discuss together such questions as: Did something happen for you? Could you share a little of how it happened? If you felt completely blocked, do you have any clues of what was blocking you? This kind of sharing can often free the blocks for some and give clues as to how to proceed to others. Try *dialoguing several times during the course in order to establish some familiarity with the method so that people can continue to use it on their own later.*

4. Listening to Music.

Select a piece of music related in some way to the material. Suggest that the group respond to the music in writing either during or immediately after the record is played. Variations of responding include working with some art media during the playing of the music or answering some specific question. Only experiencing these different activities can reveal how they become midwife to the new birth that is struggling to take place.

5. Moving to Music.

Choose a recording related to the theme and one that also invites to movement. Suggest that group members move as they feel for in response to the music. This needs to be an introverted experience, done in silence, without reference to the others in the group. If, at the outset, some are hesitant to try, suggest that they sit with closed eyes and move one foot or one hand as they feel ready to do so. If no part of the body seems willing as yet to be involved, suggest that they sit in stillness and meditate on something that has touched them in the previous discussion. This is definitely not an event to be observed but an experience to be had.

6. Responding to Pictures.

Show several pictures chosen because of their evocativeness and their relation to the text. Have the group respond either orally or in writing to two or three of the pictures. The responses, if written, need to be shared with the group at the conclusion of the writing period. The wide variety of reactions to any given picture adds new meaning to the text itself, and incidentally, is a marvelous illustration of projection.

7. Miming.

As an introduction to this type of experiment a few simple relaxing exercises can help free participants for full participation in the miming. For some people, miming is one of the most difficult of the experiments. However, if led into it by way of relaxation, they may well soon discover that acting the part can be a very significant way of moving the new insight from the mind to the substance.

Miming needs to be a very introverted experience. Often it can be done with eyes shut, or nearly shut, with the concentration being in the part one is acting. Always after such an experiment it is wise to have people articulate something of what happened in them as a result of participating.

Any one of the studies offers various opportunities for miming. For instance, in Study II, lead the group into miming such scenes as Rebekah urging Jacob into his deceptions of Esau, Jacob kneeling to receive Isaac's blessing, Esau when he discovered the deception, or Jacob in the struggle that brought his new name.

A group accustomed to lecture and discussion only may well find it rather difficult at first to move into some of these other dimensions of working on the material. However, the leader's enthusiastic conviction of the values of moving beyond discussion can help the most conservative groups into a willingness to try out these different ways of working. Successful experiences will soon convince the group of the value of approaching the material through a wide variety of channels. The purpose of all such extras must be kept in mind. It is not for the sake of doing a new thing that they are tried but for the sake of what that new technique can do to deepen the effectiveness of the selections studied.

While it would be harder for the individual working on the study by him/herself to discover the value of all of these methods, an openness to experimenting with them and a willingness to accept early frustrations if they arise could well lead to some very exciting discoveries.

Abraham, Man of Action

STUDY I

Genesis 11:27-25:10.

I. SYNOPSIS OF THE STORY.

In Genesis, the tales of the patriarchs follow the great cosmic myths, and begin Hebrew history. The questions as to whether the patriarchs ever existed as individual human beings has swung all the way from the fundamentalist position that holds to the literal truth of every word of the story as it now stands to the position that the tales are purely mythical with no foundation in facts. Some scholars lean to the position that the patriarchs might well have been actual people but that the stories about them have been so changed by oral tradition that they have almost no value as factual history. This would in no way limit their value as symbol and myth. Whatever the historic basis, the fact is that the figure of Abraham has lived throughout the ages and that he remains today an inspiring hero to Jew, Christian, and Moslem. It is to a few of the tales that have grown up around the figure of Abraham that we now turn to try to get at some of the eternal truths they contain.

Abraham first appeared on the Biblical scene when his father, Terah, moved with his family from Ur of the Chaldees to Haran. After the death of his father, Abram, as he was then called, was visited by Yahweh* who commanded: "Go from your country, and your kindred and your father's house, to the land that I will show you. And I will make of you a great nation, and I will bless you and make your name great; so that you will be a blessing. I will bless those who bless you, and him who curses you I will curse; and by you all the families of the earth will bless themselves." (Genesis 12:1-3)

So, taking all their substance and flocks, Abram, his wife, Sarai, and his nephew, Lot, set forth in obedience to Yahweh's command. With the making of the covenant with Yahweh, Abram's name was changed to Abraham, and Sarai's to Sarah. The etymology of the names is uncertain, but the new names are said to mean "the father of multitudes" and "the mother of nations."

Some of the best known stories of the Abraham saga include: Lot's choice of the more fertile land (Genesis 13); Hagar and Ishmael (Genesis 16, 17, and 21); the promise of the birth of Isaac (Genesis 16 and 17); Abraham's plea that Sodom and Gomorrah be saved (Genesis 17); the birth of

---

*In the Old Testament many different words are used to express the idea "God." Two of the earliest written sources are the "J" document, from about 950 B.C., and the "E" document, from about 850 B.C. "J" uses Yahweh (formerly Jehovah) as the chosen term for God and "E" uses Elohim. Hence the documents are identified by the author's use of the name for God.

I have chosen to use the name Yahweh throughout this text when dealing with Old Testament material. In the B questions which refer to the personal responses of the participants I have used the word God. To many Jews the name Yahweh is so sacred it is never spoken. However, to the majority of people who will use this text it will come as a relatively new term for God and will hopefully free them to discover the tremendum of the God of the Old Testament with his/her manifold opposites.

2

Isaac (Genesis 21); and Yahweh's demand for the sacrifice of Isaac with its moving denouement and deeper implications (Genesis 22).

The stress in all the tales is on Abraham's obedience and faith. He left Haran at Yahweh's command; he accepted the life of a nomad and continued his journeyings for years; he trusted the covenant even when its promise seemed impossible. The quality of all the stories is brought to a high point in the story of Abraham's response to the demand that he sacrifice Isaac, the son born to him and to Sarah in their old age, his most precious possession, the vehicle for the fulfillment of the covenant. At the moment of greatest tension Isaac was spared by Yahweh's intervention. A voice from the heavens said, "Do not lay your hand on the lad or do anything to him," and directed Abraham's gaze to a ram caught by its horns in some nearby bushes. Abraham offered the ram as a burnt offering and Isaac was spared to him. What might have been some of Abraham's feelings in such a moment? It is only as we attempt to enter the situation imaginatively that we can begin to sense its depth.

To mark his deep joy that Isaac had been spared to him, Abraham called the mount on which they stood by a Hebrew name that can be translated "The Lord Will Provide," and it is said of it to this day, "On the mount of the Lord it shall be provided."

Yahweh called out to Abraham a second time and there renewed and deepened the earlier covenant he had made with him. "By myself I have sworn, says the Lord, because you have done this and have not withheld your son, your only son, I will indeed bless you and I will multiply your descendents as the stars of the heaven and as the sand on the seashore. And your descendants shall possess the gates of their enemies and by your descendants shall all

3

the nations of the earth bless themselves because you have obeyed my voice."

II. SELECTIONS FOR STUDY

"Go from Your Country" — Genesis 12:1-9.

A. What message did Abram receive from Yahweh?
    How might he have felt on receiving such a message?
    How did he respond?
    Why did he build the altar?
    Where was it built?
    What did he do after the building of the altar?

B. What could such an inner message mean?
    Where might you hear a like message?
    (*Stay with these two questions until several different kinds of answers come from the group. For instance, a call might come to leave a specific job, a place you are living, a known activity, a given relationship, etc.*)
    How do we sometimes avoid such a command?
    Why do we hesitate?
    What kind of things can happen when the command is ignored?
    What does it take to get moving with the totality with which Abram responded?
    What do you make of the sequence: from country, from kindred, from father's house?
    How might you build an altar?
    Where might you build it?

4

Abraham Entertains Guests — Genesis 18:1-15.

A. What features of this story of nomadic hospitality impress you most?

How does Abraham respond to the visitors?

What message is brought to Sarah and to Abraham by the visitors?

How does Sarah respond to the message?

Why does she deny her laughter? (Note Abraham's similar response in Genesis 17:15-17)

B. How might an inward messenger appear today?

When such a message does arrive how is it often treated?

What could it mean to bow before the bringer of the message? To wash the messenger's feet? To supply the best of foods as refreshment?

Where might the inner Sarah laugh? (Get as many specific examples as possible of how often an inner part can laugh at the thought of new birth being a possibility.)

Isaac Is Born — Genesis 21:1-8.

A. How do we know that this child was in some way a "special child"?

What hopes are pinned on him?

How would his parents be likely to feel about him?

What two rituals are part of his infancy?

What does each signify?

5

B. What could the birth of such an inward child mean?

How might one feel at such a time?

How might we ritualize such a birth?

Why is it necessary to ritualize it?

Isaac Is Spared — Genesis 22:1-19.

(Because of its length, this section is divided into four parts. The "B" questions will come at the end of the fourth section when the story itself has been covered.)

1. Genesis 22:1-2.

A. What is Abraham asked to sacrifice?

What was the nature of Yahweh's covenant with Abraham?

How might the required sacrifice seem to effect the covenant?

How might Abraham have felt at this moment?

2. Genesis 22:3-8.

A. How does Abraham respond?

What do you gather from these verses as to Abraham's attitude to the assigned task?

Why were the two young men taken along?

What do you project into the feelings of both Abraham and of Isaac as they proceed up the mountain?

3. Genesis 22:9-14.

A. What moment in this episode moves you the most?

How do you understand the fact that Yahweh returns Isaac to Abraham?

What is the nature of Yahweh as revealed in this story?

Why do you think Abraham was able to respond as he did?

4. *Genesis 22:15-19.*

A. Why is the blessing renewed at this time?

What is the nature of the blessing?

What do you see as the next steps for Abraham? For Isaac?

B. Inner questions for this section.

What is the nature of sacrifice?

What place does sacrifice have in life today?

Where have you experienced the need to sacrifice?

What, for you, does it mean that it is the precious, the well-beloved son that is required as sacrifice?

What might that mean for you?

What would it mean to face such a sacrifice?

Symbolically, what do you make of the time — early morning? The ass? The four persons? The wood? The fire? The knife? The ram?

Even if the situation feels relatively minor in relation to the one being studied, where have you experienced the need to sacrifice something?

How might the sacrificed be unexpectedly given back to you?

How might the blessing come inwardly following the willingness to sacrifice the most precious gift?

After the blessing is given, what is the general nature of the next step?

Summary Questions.

How do you understand Abraham's relationship to the Other?

From the sections studied, what clues did you discover to help you face a need to sacrifice?

Jacob and Esau, The Twins
STUDY II

Genesis 25:30-50:33.

I. SYNOPSIS OF THE STORY.

In Abraham's old age he sent his servant back to Haran to find a wife for Isaac amongst his kinfolk. On arrival in the area, the servant met Rebekah, Abraham's niece, at the village well. They exchanged greetings as Rebekah watered his camels, and the servant discovered that she was Abraham's niece. Rebekah took the servant to Laban's tents to meet the rest of the family. Eventually after the servant made his task known, arrangements were finally completed for Rebekah to return with the servant to become the bride of Isaac.

For years Rebekah was barren. Then Isaac "prayed to the Lord for his wife because she was barren" and "the Lord granted his prayer and Rebekah his wife conceived." She bore twin sons, Jacob and Esau. Tradition has it that even in the womb there was rivalry between them. Early in their development they showed that they were very different in temperament. Esau, red and hairy from birth, was the "earth" man and became a cunning hunter; Jacob, the "plain" man, dwelt in tents and became interested in things closer to home.

While the twins were still in her womb, it became clear to Rebekah that the blessing had to move through Jacob

9

rather than through Esau, who, by right of being first born, was due to receive it at Isaac's death. Jacob bought the birthright from Esau under questionable circumstances. (See below: Genesis 25:29-34) Then, later, with his mother's help and inspiration, by trickery, he obtained his dying father's blessing. To flee Esau's wrath over the stolen blessing, Jacob, again with his mother's help, escaped to her relatives in Haran. There he lived for many years with his uncle Laban, Rebekah's brother. (Note that the possession of the blessing forced Jacob out of his mode of life into a different geographical and philosophical climate.)

Jacob fell in love with Laban's younger daughter, Rachel, and worked for Laban for seven years for the right to marry her. This time it was Jacob who was tricked, for Laban gave him Leah, the elder daughter, instead of Rachel whom he loved and for whom he had served his time. Later he was given Rachel also but he had to work another seven years for her. Following some additional years of service with Laban, and after the birth of Joseph, Rachel's first child, Jacob left with his wives, their maid-servants, his sons, the flocks earned and those achieved by trickery, and started back to Canaan.

Before he reached the end of his journey, Jacob had to meet Esau and face the problem from which he had fled long years before. In his famous struggle with the "man," Jacob saw the issue through to his own wounding and was then able to be reconciled with his brother.

II. SELECTIONS FOR STUDY.

The Birth of the Twins — Genesis 25:20-28.

A. What are the essential points of the story thus far?

What is the significance of Rachel's being barren at first?

Why does Isaac love Esau most?

Why does Rebekah favor Jacob?

How would you describe the difference between the boys?

B. What does it mean to be barren within?

What are some of the ways of treating a period of inward barrenness?

In your experience what has most helped the movement from barrenness to fertility?

What are Jacob and Esau as two opposing principles without and within?

How do you tend to show favoritism to the one or the other within you?

Esau Sells His Birthright — Genesis 25:29-34.

A. What does this episode reveal about Esau? About Jacob?

What might have been some of the reasons for Esau's being so willing to sell his birthright?

What are your reactions to Jacob's actions in this scene?

B. What could it mean inwardly that legal right to the birthright belongs to Esau?

Why must the inner Jacob receive it?

In specific, what might this mean?

11

Preparing to Steal the Blessing — Genesis 27:1-17.

A. What is Isaac's request of Esau? Why does he make such a request?

What is Esau's response to the request?

Who else heard Isaac's request? What immediate response does she make to the situation?

On what grounds does Jacob fear Rebekah's plan?

What do you make of the fact that it was Rebekah who concocted the plan?

What are the implications of "upon me be thy curse"?

("B" questions will follow the entire episode.)

Stealing the Blessing — Genesis 27:18-29.

A. What is Isaac's attitude at the beginning of this scene?

What finally convinced Isaac to give his blessing?

What do you feel to be the central ritual of the giving of the blessing?

What is the nature of the blessing?

Esau Arrives Too Late — Genesis 27:30-40.

A. What is Esau's first response to the fact of the stolen blessing?

What is Isaac's response?

What do you learn about the nature of the blessing in this scene?

What is the nature of Esau's blessing?

Jacob Leaves Home — Genesis 27:41-28:5.

A. What is Esau's plan for after Isaac's death?

How does Rebekah plan to get Jacob out of danger?

How do both Jacob and Isaac co-operate with Rebekah's plan?

What are the implications of Jacob's receiving the blessing? For Jacob? For Esau? For Rebekah?

B. Inner questions for this section: Genesis 27:1-28:5.

Who is the Isaac within?

What could it mean that Isaac is blind?

Why must the "old king" die?

What do you see as the blessing Isaac carries?

Why must that blessing be received before new life can begin?

Why must it be Jacob who receives the blessing?

What is the place of the feminine in these crucial scenes?

(Remember that the masculine and the feminine dimensions are in each individual. This does not speak of a struggle between a man and a woman but between the two dimensions within each. The story gives a chance to feel into how each works in certain situations and can be a challenge to the participants to look to the developments of both dimensions. The place of Rebekah here in the forward movement of consciousness is of critical importance.)

What are some clues for getting the better of the entrenched Isaac?

What could be the inner meaning of Jacob having to wear Esau's clothing?

What is the nature of the blessing?

How have you experienced a "blessing"? (*Even what may seem a rather minor "blessing" will, if looked at carefully, reveal many of the steps of a major transformation.*)

Jacob Dreams of the Ladder — Genesis 28:11-19a.

A. What might the dream have meant to Jacob?

What do you make of the angels ascending and descending?

Why a new covenant at this point?

Why was Jacob afraid?

Why did he build the altar?

B. What event has forced you to go on some unknown adventure?

How have you been supported at such a time?

How do you honor the spots where the help has been given?

What is the value of ritual?

How might you ritualize a moment of deep insight?

Jacob's Return to His Own Country — Genesis 32:1-23.

(*According to the story, this episode comes about a quarter of a century after the preceding tale.*)

A. How does Jacob feel as he approaches the confrontation with Esau?

How does he prepare for the meeting?

How do you feel about his preparation?

B. How do you prepare for confronting some major shadow problem?

What are some of the steps that one could take before such a confrontation?

How do you understand the giving of gifts at such a time?

Why the need to be alone before the actual face-to-face contact with the outer carrier of the shadow?

Jacob's Confrontation with the Man — Genesis 32:24-33:17.

(Verses 24-29 present a striking image of the confrontation with the other side within. In the night, alone, on the opposite side of the ford from all that he loves and all his possessions, Jacob sees it through with "the man" until "the breaking of the day." Call it dream, call it vision, call it inner confrontation, call it whatever you like, but try to sense the reality of the struggle — the wounding, the absolute need to say, "I will not let thee go except thou bless me." All this must be met inwardly before the carrier of the shadow in the outer world can be met successfully and reconciliation and healing take place.)

A. What is the nature of the struggle described here?

What is the meaning of the fact that Jacob's thigh is thrown out of joint?

Why does the "man" have to go at daybreak?

Why the new name for Jacob?

Whom does Jacob meet after crossing the ford?

Why might he now bow to Esau seven times?

What is the nature of their reunion?

15

What does Jacob receive as a result of the reconciliation?

What does Esau receive?

Why can Esau now go back to his own home?

How do you understand Jacob's saying, "I will lead on softly"?

B. What does this confrontation reveal about the inner nature of the struggle with the shadow?

Why is the wounding a necessity?

Symbolically what would it mean to have the thigh wounded?

What could it mean that the struggle came at night and ended at daybreak?

If you can, share some detail of a struggle that has preceded a reconciliation with some aspect of the shadow. What have the preceding nights been like?

What has been the nature of the struggle?

How have you experienced the inward reconciliation? The outward ones?

How have both been made possible?

What do you make inwardly of the fact that both go their own way after the reconciliation?

What is the difference now?

Summary Questions.

What aspects of the story have touched you most deeply?

What new insights have come to you that can help on your personal journey?

At what points do you feel the need for further work on the shadow, outwardly in knowledge, inwardly in experience?

(In the bibliography at the end of this course can be found material for study of the shadow. The various suggestions in the introduction under the title "Beyond Discussion" can be a help in locating specific aspects of your personal shadow.)

Joseph, The Dreamer

STUDY III

Genesis 30:22-50:26.

I. SYNOPSIS OF THE STORY.

Joseph, the eleventh son of Jacob, was the first child born to Rachel, the favorite wife. The spoiled son of an adoring older father, and the possessor of certain gifts in his own right, Joseph in time became thoroughly disliked by his older brothers. Finally, angered by his sense of superiority and his tale bearing, the brothers threw him into a pit near Dotham where they were tending their father's flocks and where Joseph had been sent to take them food. Reuben's plan to save Joseph from death worked, but his plan to return him, unharmed, to his father failed because the other brothers had meanwhile decided, on Judah's advice, to sell him to a band of Ishmaelites en route to Egypt.

Arrived in Egypt, Joseph was bought by Potiphar, a captain of the Pharoah's guard, to serve in his household. He did his work so effectively that he soon was made the overseer in charge of all the business of the estate. Later, trapped in a difficult situation by Potiphar's wife, Joseph was deprived of his office and cast into prison.

Here, too, he was diligent in the situation in which he found himself. Again he prospered and this time became the keeper of the prisoners. When he had been in prison for some time, the chief butler and the chief baker, having displeased the Pharoah, were thrown into the same prison where Joseph was kept.

One night both the butler and the baker were troubled by strange dreams which Joseph was able to interpret for them. The chief butler, as the dream foretold, was released from prison and returned to Pharoah's service. As he left the prison, he promised to speak to the Pharoah on Joseph's behalf. However, it was not until years later, when the Pharoah had a dream which his wisemen could not interpret, that the chief butler remembered his promise to Joseph, and told Pharoah of Joseph's skill in interpreting dreams.

Pharoah immediately sent for Joseph. With the help of Yahweh, Joseph interpreted Pharoah's dreams. Impressed by his skill and the message of the dreams, Pharoah made Joseph second in command in the whole land of Egypt and gave him the task of preparing the country for the seven years of severe famine that the dream had indicated would fall upon the country after seven years of plenty. By judicious planning and hard work, Joseph was able to organize the country so that new granaries were built and old ones enlarged and enough grain gathered to provide sufficient food to last through the seven years of drought.

During the course of the famine, Jacob sent his sons to Egypt for food for his starving tribesmen. Joseph recognized his brothers instantly though they did not recognize him. After a series of testing which included returning to their own country and bringing Benjamin, the youngest son, back with them, Joseph finally made himself known to them. Following a reconciliation, the brothers returned for their father, Jacob, with an invitation from the Pharoah to settle in the land of Goshen. Hence, Jacob, with his sons and all their families, their kin, and their herds returned to Egypt and settled in the land of Goshen, the northeastern section of the Nile Delta.

II. SELECTIONS FOR STUDY.

Joseph, the Favorite Son — Genesis 37:1-11.

A. How did Jacob feel about Joseph?

Why did he feel this way? (See Genesis 30:22-25)

How did Jacob show his favoritism?

How did the older brothers feel about Jacob's attitude to Joseph?

How did the brothers feel about Joseph's dreams?

What do you make of the two dreams?

How would you describe Joseph at this point in the story?

B. Who is the Joseph within you?

What is the nature of his gift?

What are the positive aspects of giving him "a special garment"?

How might you give your inner Joseph a "special garment"?

(Suggestions: a special "work" book, a cover for the book, a definite time for study, etc.)

What would such a coat symbolize?

How might it become negative?

How do your inner brothers feel about your inner Joseph?

What is the general nature of this conflict within?

How can the creative nature of the inner Joseph be nurtured?

What are some of the ways to avoid inflation over his gifts?

Joseph Sold to the Ishmaelites — 37:12-36.

A. "Here comes this dreamer." Why did the brothers hate him so?

How did they treat him on his arrival?

What did Reuben try to do?

Let your imagination encompass Joseph's reaction in the pit: stripped of his grand coat, naked, without water. What might he think? See? Feel?

(Note the confused blending of two traditions here.)

What did Judah suggest?

What did the brothers do with the coat? Why?

How did Jacob react to the loss of his favorite son?

Why did Joseph need this experience at this time?

B. What kind of inward situation is it to be put in a pit?

What is the experience of being stripped of special robes?

What does it mean inwardly to be without water?

How do we bring about negative reactions to our inward Joseph?

How do we ourselves sometimes conspire against him?

How do the elder brothers within put Joseph into a pit? How do they sell him?

Joseph Serves Potiphar — Genesis 39:1-6.

A. What happened to Joseph when he first got to Egypt?

How would you describe the new situation in which he found himself?

How did his position differ from his status at home?

What must Joseph have had to achieve to succeed in the new situations?

What is the difference between the Jacob-Joseph relationship and the Potiphar-Joseph relationship?

B. What is the inner movement from Jacob-Joseph to Potiphar-Joseph?

What are some of the steps which must be taken to move from excitement and pride over beginning experiences of the numinous within, to the "management of the household" within?

("Management" in this sense would mean the continuing effort to relate to all aspects of the unconscious which manifest themselves and not management in the sense of calling forth at will or "making it" obey.)

Joseph and Potiphar's Wife — Genesis 39:7-20.

A. What is Potiphar's wife's reaction to Joseph?

How did Joseph meet the situation?

What do you think of his solution?

How might a prison sentence prove helpful at such a point?

B. What is the nature of the feminine principle as seen here?

How have you experienced the feminine within as trying to seduce you?

How might it trap us?

How can we try to run away from it?

Why can escape be no final solution?

Since the thrust of Life is toward wholeness, what must happen regarding the masculine and feminine principles within each individual?

What might imprisonment be and mean at the point of fleeing seduction by the feminine?

Joseph in Prison — Genesis 39:21-23; 40:1-8 and 14.

A. What limitations does prison bring?

What became of Joseph in prison?

How did he approach this time of confinement?

B. What is the nature of an inner imprisonment of the Joseph figure?

What different forms can the "imprisonment" take?

How does such a period often get misused?

How can it be creatively used?

Joseph Interprets the Pharoah's Dream — Genesis 41:7b-43.

A. Why was Joseph called forth from prison?

What was the position of the Pharoah?

How did Joseph prepare himself to meet Pharoah?

What did Pharoah ask of Joseph?

How did Joseph respond to his request?

What was Pharoah's reaction to Joseph's interpretations?

Why do you think he listened to Joseph?

B.   Who is the Pharoah within?

How can we ritualize the meeting of our freed Joseph with Pharoah?

How would you describe a time of inner fullness?

How might a time of inner famine be described?

What are some positive reactions to each of these inner periods?

Why is Joseph a good inner figure to be in charge of a time of abundance? A time of famine?

What can be stored psychically?

What relation does this have to the order to gather enough manna for only one day and to the prayer, "give us this day our daily bread"?

Joseph Tests His Brothers — Genesis 42:6-25 and 44:1-13.

(The leader will need to fill in any intervening sections so the group members can sense the full drama as the story moves to reconciliation.)

A.   Why does Joseph greet his brothers so harshly?

Following the three days of imprisonment what must the brothers do? Why is Simeon kept in Egypt?

How do the brothers now feel about their treatment of Joseph?

How do you sense Joseph as feeling toward them?

What is the nature of Joseph's second test?

Why the divining cup? Why in Benjamin's sack?

What does the ruse reveal?

What, to you, most shows their change of heart?

B. What in these two episodes touches you most? Why?
Why inwardly is it necessary to test the older brothers?
Of what might such an inward testing consist?

Joseph Makes Himself Known to His Brothers — Genesis 45:1-15.

A. How do the brothers respond when Joseph makes himself known to them?

What does Joseph now feel about the original betrayal?

What are the brothers to do following their reunion with Joseph?

Why do all the brothers have to be present before the final reconciliation can take place?

Why the move of the whole family, including Jacob, to Egypt?

B. What does it mean inwardly that all the brothers have to be present before the reconciliation can take place?

How, both outwardly and inwardly, can we accept as Joseph accepted his brothers?

What lay at the root of his acceptance?

What is the nature of reconciliation?

What in specifics, would it mean to accept the inner older brothers?

What are the major steps that must precede the fact of genuine acceptance?

Summary Questions.

What do you see as Joseph's main achievements?

What kept him from inflation at each point of growth?

What to you seem the most important steps in his growth from naive young man telling his brothers his dreams to mature man, leader in time of crisis?

What for you personally was the most significant episode of those selected for study?

Why do you think it struck you so deeply?

What other insights has this study contributed to you in relation to your personal journeying?

Moses As Liberator From Bondage
STUDY IV

Exodus 1-15.

*(Moses' influence on the developing religious life of the suc-
ceeding centuries has been so important that the material
needing to be included necessitated two studies. Even so, only the
major episodes have been selected for study.)*

I. SYNOPSIS OF THE STORY.

Moses, considered by some scholars to be the first of
the historical characters in the Bible, was one of the
greatest figures in the Old Testament. Three of the world's
religions look to him as an important spiritual guide:
Judaism, Christianity, and Islam. For Judaism he was central to its whole religious development.

Tradition begins with the story of the infant preserved
from death through the ingenuity of his mother, Jochebed,
and his sister, Miriam. Born at a time when the Pharoah
had decreed the death of all male children of the Hebrews,
Moses was hidden in the bulrushes by Miriam. There he
was discovered by the Pharoah's daughter and taken to the
royal palace where he was brought up as an Egyptian.

Some time en route to manhood he must have learned
about his Hebrew heritage. In young manhood he killed an
Egyptian who was ill-treating a Hebrew. Fearing that fact
would be discovered by the Pharoah, Moses fled from the

29

court and escaped to the land of Midian. There he served the high priest of Midian and married his daughter, Zipporah.

Meantime, back in Egypt, the oppression of the children of Israel increased and their lot became more and more difficult. Yahweh, suffering over the afflictions of the Israelites, selected Moses as the one to free them from their captivity. Moses experienced Yahweh's call to him in the theophany of the burning bush. At first, hesitant and fearful, Moses tried hard to find an excuse that would relieve him of the task. In the end, he accepted his destiny under Yahweh and moved, with his brother Aaron, into the long and agonizing task to which he was called. This task had two major difficulties: that of convincing the Pharoah to allow the people to leave Egypt and the even more difficult task of arousing and maintaining the courage of those long held in bondage.

The last of the great plagues was the one where the angel of death passed over all the Hebrew homes and brought death to the eldest son in all Egyptian homes. The celebration of this event remains today a major festival of Judaism. After this last plague, the children of Israel crossed the Sea of Reeds to freedom and began the next stage of their journeying — the forty years in the wilderness.

II. SELECTIONS FOR STUDY.

The Conditions of the Israelites
Under the New Pharoah — Exodus 1:8-14.

A. Why had the children of Israel gone to Egypt in the first place?

How had their position in Egypt changed at the time of Moses' birth?

Why should they now leave?

B. Where do you have a sense of being enslaved?

Who is the Pharoah within?

How have you come to recognize your Pharoah in action?

How does he act to keep one in serfdom?

Why is it hard to break his hold?

Moses Rescued by the Pharoah's Daughter — Exodus 2:2-10.

A. Who was this baby?

Why did he have to be hidden?

How was he hidden?

What was the mother's role? Miriam's role? The Pharoah's daughter's role? *(Note the preponderance of feminine principle here.)*

B. Who is the baby Moses within?

Why must he sometimes be hidden?

What is your response to ark, pitch, and reeds?

What does the hiding mean inwardly?

Who within has the wisdom to hide him?

Why is it the feminine principle that can find the hiding place?

What could be your ark for the hiding?

Moses' Call to Leadership — Exodus 3:1-10.

A. Under what conditions did Moses hear the voice of Yahweh?

Why a bush? Why fire?

Why was it not consumed?

Why did Moses remove his shoes?

Of what was he in awe?

What was Moses called to do?

B.   What inward attitude is required to hear a call to a new task?

How do we often fail to turn aside to view the burning bush? Why?

In what ways can we take off our shoes inwardly? Ritualistically?

How can we give more place to the Moses within who stops, looks, turns toward, listens, and responds?

Moses' First Responses to Yahweh's Call — Exodus 3:11-15 and 4:1-15.

A.   How did Moses respond at first?

What lay back of the question: "Who am I that I should go?"

What is the significance of Moses' question in Exodus 3:13?

What do you make of Yahweh's answer in Exodus 3:14?

What was Moses seeking in Exodus 4:1-9?

(If time permits, the symbolism in these nine verses could be dealt with, but this might deflect from the mainstream of development and could prove a trap.)

What was Moses' last stand against Yahweh?

Why do we sometimes fear articulation?

Who was Aaron?

Why was he needed?

B. Why do we draw back from what seems to be a God-given task?

Which of Moses' responses hit you the hardest?

How has your favorite withdrawal response held you back from your task?

Under what circumstances might a similar dialogue happen inwardly?

The First Encounter with Pharoah — Exodus 5:17-23.

A. When the demand for freedom is made what is the first reaction of Pharoah? of the children of Israel? of Moses?

Why does Pharoah increase the difficulties at this point?

B. How have you experienced this reaction from your inner Pharoah? How has no straw been given?

Why is it so hard to get away from him?

Pharoah's Response to the Plague of Flies — Exodus 8:25-28.

A. Why can the sacrifices not be made within the land of Egypt?

What does Pharoah finally grant at this point?

How do you understand his change of heart?

B. Inwardly, why might one go on a three-day journey into the wilderness?

What might such a journey mean to you?

How might one experience the "only ye shall not go very far away"?

In specifics, how can the inward Pharoah work to hold us in bondage?

How have you sensed the tyrant part within longing for its own healing?

Further Encounters with the Pharoah — Exodus 10:7-11 and 21-26.

A. What does Moses demand that they be allowed to take with them?

What part of their demands does Pharoah grant this time?

What further does he grant after three days of "thick darkness"?

Why does Moses persist in his first demands?

B. What does it mean inwardly that all must be freed?

How do we suffer with the women in bondage? With the little ones in bondage? With the flocks and herds in bondage?

The Death of the Firstborn of Egypt — Exodus 12:1-13 and 28-34.

A. What was the nature of the last plague?

How were the Israelites to prepare for the event?

Why "loins girded," "sandals on your feet," and "staff in your hand"?

What was Pharoah's reaction? The Egyptian reaction to the death of their firstborn?

B.   What could it mean inwardly to be so prepared for the break from slavery?

What inward meaning can you sense in putting the sign of blood on the threshold?

Why must the inward Pharoah lose his eldest son?

Crossing the Sea of Reeds — Exodus 14:5-31 and 15:1-2, 20-22.

A.   How did the Israelites react to the pursuit of the Egyptians?

How does Moses react?

How does Yahweh react to Moses' petition?

What happened to the Egyptian army?

What happened to the children of Israel?

What is their immediate response to their release?

Who is Miriam? What is the nature of her song?

B.   What kind of inner situation is this?

What does it mean to you to cross a sea?

Why can it not happen until the break with Pharoah?

What does it mean that the Egyptian army arrived at the moment when success was close at hand?

Where might you hear the equivalent of "Speak to the children of Israel that they go forward"?

In what different ways have you ritualized a psychic victory?

Why is it important to acknowledge victory with "timbrel, song, and dance"?

Summary Questions and Suggestions.

(Since the struggle with the inner tyrant is a major one on the personal journey, and since this material presents it so graphically, it would be well to spend time looking back on some of the specifics that have come from the discussion.)

In how many different ways have you seen the Pharoah at work?

How does the Pharoah grant something and then, when the plague is removed, go back on his word?

What can happen when a symptom disappears and relative comfort returns to body and psyche?

How do the enslaved parts co-operate with Pharoah at such a time?

What ways have you discovered to help keep you in touch with the inner Moses who can lead to freedom and new life?

(This would be an excellent study to try an experiment in dialogue. Moses' dialogue with Yahweh in the early part of the study illustrates one possibility. However, for many people, to begin by trying to dialogue with the Other would be too much for a first attempt. To dialogue with the Pharoah part of the psyche is likely to prove considerably easier. A twenty minute period where each one tries to get in touch with his/her own inner Pharoah in written dialogue could be a very creative part of this study. Remember the dialogues themselves are not to be shared, but a brief time of talking of how it worked and what blocks there were could be fruitful for all.)

Moses As Leader in The Wilderness
STUDY V

Exodus 19:10-34:11; Numbers 20:1-13 and 27:12-22;
Deuteronomy 34:1-10.

I. SYNOPSIS OF THE STORY.

Study IV dealt with the Moses material through to the safe crossing of the Sea of Reeds and the joyful celebration of that victory. Then followed the period of forty years in the wilderness before entering the Promised Land. (The "forty" is not an exact figure but, as often in the Bible, means "a long time.") There are several theories as to the route the Israelites took through the wilderness. One thing is certain: the movement from the very beginning was not an easy one. The people cried out again and again to go back to the slavery of Egypt rather than to suffer the hardships of wilderness life. Early came the question of food. As non-desert people they did not recognize that manna was good for food. When they were educated to its use as such some tried to ignore Moses' instructions and take more than a day's share, but they soon discovered the futility of such disobedience. Frequently came the need for water, and often at such times the people forgot their hopes and complained bitterly against Moses, Aaron, and Yahweh.

"On the third new moon after leaving Egypt" the people came into the wilderness of Sinai to the foot of the Mount of God. This mount, sometimes called Sinai, sometimes Horeb, cannot be located with any surety today. Claims are made for three different mountains, but many scholars feel that this is one fact about which we can never be sure. Such theories about the actual site deal with an extraneous question. What matters is that we grapple with the meaning of the Sinai experience. It is the traditional site of the major covenant between Yahweh and his chosen people. All their history in the three millenia since that time looks back to the fact that Yahweh led them to freedom and made his covenant with them at Sinai.

In the wilderness period began the coming together of the people into some sense of community. Their suffering, while discouraging at points and causing open rebellion at others, still overall brought the people closer together and into some sense of a destiny that was theirs as a people. Only as a united people could they begin to establish themselves in Caanan.

The major stories in the Book of Exodus are two: the escape from Egypt, and the giving of the Law. One cannot be sure of any sequence of events during the wilderness period. In the light of today's idea of history there is no record of the years in the wilderness. One thing stands out — that is the figure of Moses caring, directing, interceding for the people, becoming angry and frustrated but always carrying on. He was the fiery, spiritual leader of his people, meeting Yahweh on the mount, in the tent of the Tabernacle, bringing Yahweh's message to the everyday life of the people during the wilderness years.

Study V deals mainly with some of the earliest traditions about giving of the Law and its acceptance as part of the Covenant between Yahweh and the Israelites.

II. SELECTIONS FOR STUDY.

Preparation for Yahweh's Descent — Exodus 19:10-15.

A. What makes you feel that this preparation is for a major event?

What step in the preparation impresses you most?

Why are the boundaries essential?

B. Symbolically, why a three-day preparation period?

How do you prepare when you sense something about to come to fruition?

What are some of the things that need to be done in order to meet the Other?

What do you sense as the inward need to maintain a certain distance from the mountain?

Yahweh's Descent — Exodus 19:16-25.

A. In spirit join with the people as Moses brought them "out of the camp to meet God":

What is the nature of the event dealt with in these verses?

What did the people see? Hear?

What might they have felt? Expected?

Walk with Moses to his meeting with Yahweh:

Why do you think Yahweh sent him down again to warn the people to keep their distance?

Toward what is all this preparation leading?

B. *(Though this is a tremendum experience that may happen rarely, if ever, for most individuals, don't let that be an escape from personal issues. Less dramatic times, too, bring about important new steps on our journeys.)*

How have you inwardly experienced thunder, lightning, smoke, fire, earthquake?

What has helped you meet such a time?

How can we cultivate our relationship with the Moses within who can walk through the thick darkness to meet with Yahweh?

(Traditionally, the Commandments were given on Mount Sinai, and in this text they follow immediately on the above episode. More about the meaning of the covenant, its ritual acceptance, the history of "covenant" through the Old Testament will be included in a second Old Testament course to follow. Here we move to the story about Moses' descent from the mountain bearing the tablets of the Law.)

The Golden Calf —
Exodus 32:1-6, 7-14, 15-20, and 30-34.

A. What is the situation back in the camp while Moses is still on the mountain top?

How does Yahweh respond to this situation?

What is Moses' reaction to Yahweh's anger?

What was Moses' reaction when he went back to the camp?

B. Where have you sensed impatience turning you aside from a major creative decision?

How do we build idols instead of waiting for God's Law?

How do we hear: "But now go lead the people to the place of which I have spoken to you"?

Moses Returns to the Mount — Exodus 34:1-11a.

A. How might Moses have felt in returning to the mount with the two blank stones?

How do you visualize this meeting between Moses and Yahweh?

What does Moses petition of Yahweh?

B. What can happen inwardly following an episode that destroys a central religious effort?

In this section, what clues are given that made possible the next step forward?

The Ten Words — Exodus 20:2-17.

(Remember that the Mosaic code is central to the development and life of Judaism. That these commandments be obeyed if Yahweh is to keep his side of the covenant is the heart of the Mosaic covenant.)

A. How can adherence to the commandments keep an open pathway between Yahweh and individuals?

How are they basic to personal relationships?

How might they be misused?

What does it mean that Yahweh has given the Law?

B. What does it mean inwardly that there is a God-given Law?

What makes for this law being a living experience?

What happens when we try to escape the Divine Imperative?

The Covenant Is Sealed — Exodus 24:3-8.

A. Why is there the pre-ritual step of verse three?

(Note that two traditions from the earliest materials are contained in this chapter. The second has been chosen for our study. Open yourself to imaginative participation in this dramatic ritual.)

What is the first step in the ritual itself?

Why the altar? The pillars? At the foot of the mountain?

Why the sacrifices of the oxen?

What is the importance of "blood"?

What do you feel as central in the blood thrown at the altar?

Why the ritual of the reading at this particular point?

What do you feel is the meaning of the second half, the blood being thrown on the people?

B. *Rather than discuss the inward implications of such a deeply stirring ritual it is recommended that time be given in the session itself to allow people to move into writing answers to the following questions:*

What is the nature of the covenant that God wants to make with you at this point in your life?

Are you willing to accept the terms of the covenant?

How might you ritualize your acceptance when it is achieved?

(In this case there should be no sharing of the experience. The reason for starting the writing during the group session is to begin a personal response under the immediate impact of the work on the material. Obviously, it will not be completed within the time that can be alloted to it, but some of the spirit of the session will be caught in an immediate answer and can be picked up in further work on it at home.)

Moses and the Waters of Meribah — Numbers 20:1-13.

A. What is the attitude of the people in verses 2-5?

What is the first step Moses and Aaron take after hearing the sullen protestations of the people?

What was the nature of their experience in the tent of meeting?

What was Moses' attitude in striking the rock?

What was Yahweh's response to Moses' action?

What do you feel to be the sin in the response: "Hear now ye rebels, must we fetch you water out of the rock?"

What had entered Moses' spirit that makes Yahweh declare that Moses shall not enter the promised land?

B. Search out your inner response when everything seems to be wrong.

What is a first step out of the situation?

When a clue for solution of a central point of stress has come, what are some of the errors we can make?

How can we strike the rock and bring forth God's anger?

Moses' Death — Numbers 27:12-22 and Deuteronomy 34:1-10.

A. What in Moses made it possible for him to participate in the ritual dedication of the new leader?

What do you fantasy Moses as feeling as he surveyed the Promised Land?

43

B. Does any given inner figure ever reach its full possibility? Why or why not?

What are some of the specific ways you have worked to accept the fact that a given goal must now be relinquished?

Summary Questions.

What has this study added to your understanding of Moses? To your appreciation of him?

How has it deepened your knowledge about the personal journey?

With what episode in either study did you find it hardest to deal?

Which episode is most vividly alive in you at this moment? Why?

Stories From The Life of David
STUDY VI

I Samuel 16-18 and II Samuel 12.

I. INTRODUCTORY STATEMENT.

David's reign was of major importance to the political, social, and religious life of the United Kingdom. Obviously he needed to be included among the individuals to be studied. However, it does not seem advisable to include a series of studies on the whole Davidic era but instead choose three well-known stories about David for group study.

The material about David found in Samuel I and II illustrates the frankness of the Old Testament in preserving a well rounded picture of its heroes. David was the great hero king above and beyond any other, and yet, side by side with the stories of his greatness, there are stories of his weakness. In much Old Testament material there is no attempt to make the struggling human being a faultless person. This very inclusion of the opposites makes for the psychological authenticity of the stories and their relevancy for our day.

II. BRIEF OUTLINE OF DAVID'S REIGN.

David, youngest son of Jesse, of the tribe of Judah, tended his father's flocks in the Judean hills. The sources give differing accounts of how David got to Saul's court, but get there he did and was for a time in high favor with Saul. Eventually, however, David's successes in battle roused Saul's jealously, and David had to flee the court and, later, leave the country. The Philistine king, Achish, granted David the frontier town of Ziglag in return for David's help against marauders in the area.

At the death of Saul, David returned and was appointed king of Judah. He settled in Hebron and established his court there. For some years Ishbosheth, Saul's son, reigned in Israel and opposed David's claim to the kingship of the northern kingdom. Though against David's will and command, Abner, Ishbosheth's chief captain, and later, Ishbosheth himself, were both murdered by David's men. David gave both proper burial and punished the murderers with death. After Ishbosheth's death, all opposition to David came to an end, and he was annointed king over all twelve tribes.

Besides the acquisition of considerable territory and the establishment of peace, David's reign is also noted for the choice of Jerusalem as the capital city. Originally a fortress owned by the Jebusites, Jerusalem was captured by David. After its capture, David decided to move his capital there. This was an astute move. It was a strong fortress centrally located on neutral ground that had never belonged to either the southern or the northern kingdom. The city grew steadily in importance until it became a great spiritual and political center. Today it is not only a great spiritual center for millions of people of differing faiths but a center of intense political import. Symbolically, it stands for the "Holy City," "the New Jerusalem," the "Spiritual Center" toward which one moves and from which one receives the power to move.

(For a brief report on David's relationship to the Book of Psalms see Study XII.)

III. SELECTIONS FOR STUDY.

DAVID AND SAUL:

David at the King's Court — I Samuel 16:14-23.

A. How would you describe Saul at this point in his career?

Why did he need David?

How do you picture David here?

How did Saul react to David?

How did David respond?

What is the nature of Yahweh who sends the evil spirits as well as the good?

B. How might we be troubled by an "evil spirit from the Lord"?

How can one begin to deal with such a state?

What difference could it make to accept the evil spirit as coming from the Lord?

What methods similar to Saul's might help?

Who is the Saul within you?

What would it mean for him to have an armor bearer?

Who is the David within?

How can one keep in touch with him?

47

David Meets Saul's Jealousy — I Samuel 18:5-16.

A. How did Saul come to regard David?

Why did the jealousy develop?

How do you feel about Saul's attack on David?

How did David react to the situation?

B. What is jealousy like?

What does it do to the one who is jealous?

What are some effective ways to deal with it in outer relationships?

Inwardly, how can one part of ourselves become jealous of another? How might some new development make for jealousy on the part of the old king?

If growth is to continue, why does the old king have to yield to the new?

What happens when the old king succeeds in murdering the new?

When and how have you thrown a javelin at your David?

How can one help the inner old king to accept the new?

DAVID AND GOLIATH:

David's Response to a Challenge — I Samuel 17:3-11, 16-26.

A. What scene is described here?

Who is Goliath?

What was his challenge?

How did Saul's army react to this challenge?

What new element entered the scene with the arrival of
David?

Why had David come?

What was his response to the situation he found?

B. Describe an inner situation where two opposing forces
are lined up to do battle.

What is the nature of an inner giant?

How do you respond to giants?

How might such a giant paralyze your inner movement
as Goliath paralyzed the army of Israel?

If you could hear your inner David at such a moment,
what might he be saying?

What are some of the ways in which we can keep in
closer touch with the inner David who brings sus-
tenance from the father?

Recall the last "gigantic" task you had to do. How did
you respond when challenged? What happened if you
did not accept? How did you achieve the victory if you
won?

David's Eldest Brother Enters the Scene —
I Samuel 17:28-29.

A. How did David's brother respond to David's comments?

What specific accusations did he make against David?

How do you feel about this scene?

How did David respond to Eliab?

B. Where have you felt the condemnation of an inward
eldest brother?

What possible reactions are there to such an attack?

(First responses may well be to an outer brother. Stay there for a time, if it seems wise to do so, but be sure to move also to the inner one.)

David Refuses Saul's Armor — I Samuel 17:32-40.

A. How did David respond to the task to which he felt called?

Why did he refuse Saul's armor?

B. How does one feel when confident about the next task?

When such confidence is warranted, from whence does it come?

Why must one refuse another's armor at such a time?

What happens when one tries to use another's armor?

(Specific illustrations of how we try to do this can be invaluable here, in making clear the point at issue.)

The Death of Goliath — I Samuel 17:41-51.

A. How did Goliath feel about David?

How did David feel as he faced Goliath?

What was the result of the fight?

B. How does the inner Goliath feel in relation to an encounter with the inner David?

Why is it essential that we stay in touch with the inner David?

What happens when we are cut off from David?

DAVID CONFRONTS HIS SIN:

(From his rooftop, David viewed Bathsheba, the beautiful wife of Uriah, bathing and sent for her to come to him. When Bathsheba became pregnant from this union, David, failing to get Uriah home to sleep with his wife, sent word to his captain, Joab, to see that Uriah was placed in the front line of battle where he would surely be killed.)

The Prophet Challenges the King — II Samuel 12:1-15.

A. What is the injustice in the story told by Nathan?

   How did David react to the story?

   Why did Nathan tell the story?

   How could the prophet dare challenge the king?

   What does this episode tell of Nathan? Of David?

   How did David react to the statement "You are the man"?

   Why can repentance and forgiveness not blot out all results?

   Why do you feel the child must die?

B. Inwardly, what might it mean that it is the king who steals and kills?

   In what kind of situation might we hear the accusation, "You are that person"?

   What might repentance mean in regard to an inner situation?

   How do you understand "The Lord also has put away your sin . . . Nevertheless the child that is born to you shall die"?

David's Action Before and After the Child's Death — II Samuel 12:15b-24.

A. How did David act during the child's illness?

Why did he act in this manner?

How did David act after the death of the child?

How do you feel about his change of attitude here?

How might he have reacted?

B. What can it mean inwardly to acknowledge "I have sinned against the Lord"? To fast? To lie all night upon the earth? To have the child die?

Following the death of the child, what would it mean to arise from the earth? To wash? To annoint oneself? To go into one's house and eat? To have intercourse with the one whose child has died?

In other words, what does it mean to accept the sin with all its consequences, yet to move forward totally into the future?

Summary Questions.

What opposites are expressed in each of the episodes of the study?

What incident speaks most deeply to your current psychic need?

What is the most difficult thing for you to accept as part of your own journey?

Confrontation With Yahweh

STUDY VII

Amos 7:12-17; Isaiah 6:1-8; Jeremiah 1:4-10, 17-19.

I. BACKGROUND MATERIAL.

The works of the three prophets whose calls are being dealt with are the three prophetic books bearing their names: Amos, Isaiah, and Jeremiah. Amos was the earliest of the writing prophets, and the book of Amos was possibly the first book of the Old Testament to be written in its present form. The book of Isaiah is a compilation of prophetic writings gathered around two or three major figures. The work of Isaiah of Jerusalem is to be found in chapters 1-39 of the book, and even within those chapters there are later additions. The book of Jeremiah can be divided into three main sections: the words of Jeremiah, Baruch's biography of Jeremiah, and the oracles against foreign nations. Within the book are sections written by later hands, and Biblical scholars have been unable to agree as to what can be attributed to Jeremiah himself. In general the words of Jeremiah and the material about him attributed to Baruch are considered reliable source material by most scholars.

Working with the prophets, we are plunged into the political, economic, and social life of a people. By some scholars, Moses is considered to be the first historical person in the Old Testament. Many of the stories about him are legendary, but behind the traditions that have grown

53

around him stands an individual human being and a great leader. David was, without question, a historical person, and we have much factual detail from his times included along with folk tale and legend. With the prophets one moves into the historical scene. Their dialogues with Yahweh and their efforts, rising out of that dialogue, to make people face the social and religious issues of their day make their work particularly relevant to our day.

The peak of Israel's religious development was the age of the great prophets. Elijah and Elisha, the forerunners of the age, were followed by a succession of outstanding men whose work spanned the years from approximately 760 B.C. to 525 B.C. After the return from Exile the great prophetic line disappeared and religion became more circumscribed.

One way to glimpse the nature of the prophetic task is to compare it with the apocalyptic era that followed. In the apocalyptic view, the human could play no part. The new creation was to be brought into being by an act of God following the destruction of the existing age in some sort of holocaust. Since, according to the apocalyptists, no act of humans could change the Divine Will, they brought no moral or ethical judgment to daily actions. (See Martin Buber's article, "Prophecy, Apocalyptic, and the Historical Hour" in *Pointing the Way*, for a brief development of this point.) In contrast to this approach, the prophet called persons to decision in each particular moment. From his confrontations with Yahweh, the prophet took to the people the message he had received. With urgent insistency, they called people to repent and return to Yahweh, for they believed that if people turned to Yahweh and chose his ways again, the course of history could be changed. They were deeply involved in the living issues of their day and spoke with passion to the need for change. From the vast richness of material, three key passages have been selected.

Each has to do with a prophet's confrontation with Yahweh at the moment when he was called to his task of prophetic leadership.

II. SELECTIONS FOR STUDY

(A brief synopsis of the prophet's work will follow the discussion of the passage on his call to this mission. This material will follow rather than precede the discussion so that the group may glimpse what it meant to each of the men to accept his destiny as a prophet of Yahweh.)

AMOS' CALL

**Amos Tells of His Call to Be a Prophet —
Amos 7:14-15.**

A. What comes to mind when you think of a shepherd?

   What was Amos doing when the Lord "took" him?

   What do you think "took him" means?

   How do you feel about that phrase?

   Why do you think Amos was open to hear the call?

   Why do we often fail to hear the call?

   Under what circumstances do we expect it?

   When did Amos hear it?

   What can that say to us?

B. Who is the Amos within who can hear and answer the call?

   If it is the shepherd quality that can hear and respond how can we develop that quality in our lives?

What might have to be sacrificed to develop it?

Having once heard it, how do we often forget it? Why?

Amos Faces Amaziah — Amos 7:12-13 and 16-17.

A. Who is Amaziah?

Why did he send Amos away?

How did Amos respond to Amaziah's command?

Why is it shocking that it is Amaziah who won't listen to the word of Yahweh?

B. Who is Amaziah within?

How do we generally think of him?

Why can't he hear the prophetic word?

Give illustrations of where the most "officially" religious within has failed to hear the prophet's word.

AMOS

Amos, a native of Judah, prophesied in Israel during the latter half of the reign of Jeroboam I, king of Israel from 784 B.C. to 745 B.C. This was a period of the revival of Israel's strength and included military successes, extension of territory, and a period of prosperity which brought a false sense of security that helped lead to the nation's downfall in 722 B.C. With the development of an urban economy came the accompanying social problems — power in the hands of the wealthy, exploitation of the poor, formal religion, and moral dissolution.

Amos was a powerful, fiery, courageous, "speaker forth" for Yahweh against the developing social evils. In no uncertain terms he warned the people against perversion of justice, dishonesty, laziness, living in luxury at the expense of the poor. The whole book is a strident, fearless call to justice and a true religion. His message is perhaps best summarized in the following passage in which Yahweh speaks through Amos:

> "I hate, I despise your feasts,
>> and I take no delight in your solemn assemblies.
> Even though you offer me your burnt offerings and
>> cereal offerings
>> I will not accept them
> And the peace offerings of your fatted beasts
>> I will not look upon them.
> Take away from me the noise of your songs;
>> to the melody of your harps I will not listen.
> But let justice roll down like waters,
>> and righteousness like an everflowing stream."
>> —Amos 5:21-24

ISAIAH'S CALL

"In the Year that King Uzziah Died" — Isaiah 6:1a.

A. How would you describe situations that could arise at the death of a strong king?

Why might Isaiah have gone to the temple?

Why might a vision come at such a time?

B. What could be the inner meaning of the death of a king following a long successful reign? Give several different examples so that the tremendous impact of such an experience can be felt and understood.

How do we try to avoid acknowledging the fact that such a death has in reality taken place?

What might be the nature of the temple to which you would turn?

Why is a "temple" needed at such a time?

Isaiah's Experience — Isaiah 6:1b-4.

A. What are "seraphim"?

Why do they cover their faces?

What aspect of God is Isaiah facing here?

How do you respond as you feel into his experience?

B. What kind of inward experience is described here?

In what kind of situation has your soul responded, "holy, holy, holy"? How does awe affect you? What follows an awe-filled experience?

How have you felt an inward earthquake?

(This is a major, dramatic turning point experience. Group members may feel far from such a "tremendum," but each has, in some way, had an experience of "shattering," and the sharing of such experiences can help people see the breadth of ways in which God speaks to persons.)

Isaiah's Response — Isaiah 6:5-8.

A. What is Isaiah's first response to "having seen the King, the Lord of Hosts"?

Why unclean lips?

In your own words describe this purging experience.

Why the burning coal?

Why on the mouth?

How does it purge?

What happens following the cleansing?

How does Isaiah feel about accepting his task?

B. Where have we unclean lips? (Give as many personal illustrations as possible so that this can be seen for what it is — one of the central problems of our day.)

How might we experience a cleansing? A call to a new task?

How do you most frequently respond to any new task?

What most speaks to you from Isaiah's vision?

ISAIAH

Isaiah of Jerusalem was an aristocrat, who had access to kings and councillors and was acquainted with the temple and temple affairs. He lived from 765 B.C. to 690 B.C. He was married, had two sons, and a group of disciples. Uzziah's reign (783-742 B.C.) was long and prosperous and included territorial conquests, improved fortifications, and the growth of social evils attendant upon prosperity. The period left the kingdom unprepared for the hard times that were to come. An alliance of Syria and Israel attacked Judah in 783 B.C., and though Judah was able to turn them back it was but a temporary respite. Israel fell to Assyria in 722 B.C., and while Judah survived, she became a vassal state of Assyria.

Isaiah's call came to him at the time of Uzziah's death in 742 B.C. For more than forty years of growing unrest he worked in the city of Jerusalem. He preached against alliances with any of the foreign powers and forsaw the downfall of Jerusalem itself if the people did not change their ways. He stressed the supremacy and holiness of Yahweh and called continually for justice and repentance. With the world around him falling apart, Isaiah yet believed that Jerusalem could be saved if the people repented, turned back to Yahweh, and followed his commandments. A few verses from Chapter 1 will serve to sum up some of his central teaching as follows:

> "When you come to appear before me
>> who requires of you
>> this trampling of my courts?
> Bring no more vain offerings;
>> incense is an abomination to me.
> New moon and sabbath and the calling of assemblies —
>> I cannot endure iniquity and solemn assembly.
> Your new moons and your appointed feasts
>> my soul hates;
> they have become a burden to me,
>> I am weary of bearing them.
> When you spread forth your hands
>> I will hide my eyes from you;
> And even though you make many prayers
>> I will not listen;
>> your hands are full of blood.
> Wash yourselves; make yourselves clean;
>> remove the evil of your doings from before my eyes;
> cease to do evil,
>> learn to do good;
> seek justice,
>> correct oppression;
> defend the fatherless,
>> plead for the widow.
>
>> —Isaiah 1:12-17

JEREMIAH'S CALL

Jeremiah's First Response to Yahweh's Call — Jeremiah 1:4-6.

A. What is the nature of Yahweh's approach to this man?

   How does Jeremiah respond?

B. Out of what kind of experience does the feeling of being known come?

   How do we say "I am only a youth"?

   Why do we fear to grow up?

Yahweh's Response to Jeremiah's Fears — Jeremiah 1:7-10.

A. How does Yahweh respond to Jeremiah's withdrawal?

   Why does the Lord touch his mouth?

   How does this ritual differ from the comparable one with Isaiah?

   What significance do you feel from the fact that it was Yahweh himself who touched Jeremiah's lips?

   What is Jeremiah's task to be?

   Why four "rootings out" to two "buildings up"?

B. How does this experience of Jeremiah's speak to you?

   How might the Lord touch an individual's lips today?

   What must be rooted out?

   What must be built up?

   Why is it difficult to root out? To build up?

The Visions and the Renewal of Yahweh's Promise
Jeremiah 1:11-19.

A. What do these verses add for Jeremiah in his situation?

B. What might it mean for you to hear: "Gird up your loins; arise"?

What do you feel to be the next step to which destiny is calling you?

How might you experience, "I am with thee, saith the Lord"?

JEREMIAH

Jeremiah was active from 625 B.C. to 585 B.C. These four decades were chaotic and crucial for the kingdom of Judah. It was the period of the complete triumph of Babylon. Nineveh fell to Babylon in 612 B.C. Egypt was defeated at Carcemish in 604 B.C., and Judah was taken in 597 B.C. and made a vassal state. Later, in 587 B.C., following an attempted insurrection, Jerusalem itself was destroyed, and many more people were sent into exile than had been sent during the first deportation of 597 B.C.

Jeremiah was a deeply sensitive man who felt the constant pressure of Yahweh's prodding him to speak forth against alliances with Egypt and for genuine religion, truth, justice, and the maintenance of the relationship with Yahweh. Personally his was a lonely life, for at Yahweh's behest he was to have no wife and no social intercourse with families at times of mourning or of rejoicing. Fleming James has said of him in *Personalities of the Old Testament* the following: "Heavy indeed was the duty of isolation laid upon the sociable and very human Jeremiah but he assumed it sternly and fulfilled it." We know more about his inner life and struggles than we do of those of anyone else in Old Testament writing. Among other materials, we have the records of several of his confrontations with Yahweh. These bring us very close to the heart of the man and reveal the roots of his faith. He has been called a prophet of doom because it was he who had to proclaim that Jerusalem itself would fall to the enemy. We find the heart of his message in Jeremiah 31:31-34 as follows:

> "Behold the days are coming, says the Lord, when I will make a new covenant with the house of Israel and the house of Judah, not like the covenant which I made with their fathers when I took them by the hand to bring them out of the land of Egypt, my covenant which they broke, though I was their husband, says the Lord. But this is the covenant which I will make with the house of Israel after those days, says the Lord. I will put my law within them and I will write it upon their hearts; and I will be their God, and they shall be my people. And no longer shall each man teach his neighbor and each his brother, saying, 'Know the Lord,' for they shall all know me, from the least of them to the greatest, says the Lord; for I will forgive their iniquity, and I will remember their sin no more."
>
> —Jeremiah 31:31-34

Summary Questions.

A. What is the nature of Yahweh's call to each of these three men?

Wherein are their experiences similar?

Where do they differ?

How would you compare and contrast the response of each man?

B. Which of the three experiences spoke most directly to your need?

How does God confront men and women today?

What is essential if one is to hear the call?

How have you felt a challenge to a specific task?

What clues have you discovered that help you to differentiate God's voice from other voices that may speak in you?

What are some of the ways you help yourself move from vision to action?

The Creation Stories

STUDY VIII

Genesis 1-3.

I. GENERAL BACKGROUND MATERIAL.

Creation myths are widespread. Everywhere primitive humanity turned to the surroundings and pondered on the beginnings of earth, sky, and sea; sun, moon, and stars; animal, bird, and beast. From the immediate area of Palestine have come different creation myths including the Summerian, the Assyrian, the Hittite, and the Babylonian. One can see the influence of the Babylonian story on the Biblical tale, but the Old Testament stories have their own inner core that distinguishes them from the neighboring accounts. *(Note the two different accounts in Genesis: 1-2:4a and 2:4b-3:24. The second tale comes from a very early tradition and was written in its present form long before the first-told tale was written.)*

Because myth touches the inner depths and speaks to the heart in a very special way, it can be most fruitful to a further understanding of the self. In *A Magic Dwells*, Dr. Moon has followed the development of the Navajo Indian Creation myth. In relation to our present study, it is interesting to note that in the Navajo myth the feminine wisdom from the depth brought the new creation, whereas in the Biblical myth, the masculine spirit from above moved into the darkness that covered the earth. Pondering that difference, what do you see as a western cultural task for our day?

The Biblical Creation story touches so deeply into the God-human relationship that it, along with the two other cosmic myths found in the early chapters of Genesis, have been left to follow the studies on the individuals. The group by now has experienced the method and will also have begun to sense the fact that various characters and situations are alive inside each person. Only after such an introduction is one prepared to grapple with the Biblical story of creation.

II. SYNOPSIS OF STORY.

Since the stories are short enough to be read within the group session, no summary of the material will be given here.

III. SELECTIONS FOR STUDY.

Before working with any specific sections have the later story, Genesis 1-2:4a, read aloud that all may re-experience its majestic sweep.

Introductory Questions.

How do you react to the word "Creation"?

What images does it bring to you?

What thoughts does it arouse?

Creation of Heaven-Earth, Day-Night — Genesis 1:1-5.

A. How does this scene make you feel?

What pictures come to mind?

What comes to change the scene?

How do you envision the movement of the spirit of God upon the waters?

What were the first words said by Yahweh?

What is your personal reaction to this first day of creation?

B. What inward situation is comparable to the time of "void and darkness"?

How have you experienced the movement of the spirit of God at such a period?

What does light symbolize?

How might one experience its coming?

How can the birth of light transform a situation?

Give specific illustrations.

The Creation of Humankind — Genesis 1:26-28.

A. In this verison of the creation story, how was the human created?

What tasks were given to him?

How do you understand "male and female created he them"?

What does it say of the nature of Yahweh?

B. What are some of the characteristics of the feminine dimension? Of the masculine dimension?

How would you interpret the statement that "both dimensions are present in every human being"?

Why is it important to recognize the opposites in your own being and to give both a chance for creative expression?

What can happen when any opposite is unrecognized or unacknowledged?

The Garden of Eden and the Creation of Eve — Genesis 2:8-10; 15-25.

(This and the following selections are from the more primitive tale.)

A. How would you describe the garden?

  What is the difference between the two trees?

  What tasks does Yahweh give to the man here?

  What is the nature of Yahweh, the Creator, in this tale?

  Why does he forbid the man to eat from the tree of knowledge of good and evil?

  How would you describe conditions in the garden at the end of chapter 2?

  What, if anything, do you feel to be missing from the scene?

  Why are the man and the woman not yet ashamed?

B. What does a garden symbolize for you?

  What does it mean that the tree of the knowledge of good and evil is planted there from the beginning?

  What kind of situation is comparable to being in a Garden of Eden?

  What is lacking in the situation?

  How do we often try to stay in our particular Garden of Eden?

The Serpent Tempts Eve — Genesis 3:1-7.

A. With what did the serpent confront Eve?

Why did he thus confront her?

Who is the serpent? From whence did he get his wisdom?

What is the relation between Yahweh and the serpent?

Why does the serpent go to Eve and not to Adam?

What happened as a result of eating the fruit?

What did it mean to them to have their eyes opened?

(The B questions will follow the remainder of the sections.)

Adam and Eve Confronted by Yahweh — Genesis 3:8-21.

A. Why did they hide themselves from Yahweh?

Of what were they ashamed?

How did Adam try to explain the situation?

How did Yahweh respond to their act of disobedience?

What is the curse put on the serpent? The woman? The man?

How do you understand the fact that Yahweh clothed them before he sent them from the Garden?

Adam and Eve Sent from the Garden — Genesis 3:22-24.

A. Why did Yahweh expel them from the garden of Eden?

To what task did he send them?

Why did Yahweh protect the garden? How?

Why the Cherubim? Why the flaming sword?

B. (For the three preceding sections)

What does it mean to eat of the fruit of the tree of the knowledge of good and evil?

What is sacrificed by eating of the fruit?

What is gained by the disobedience?

What does it mean inwardly that the serpent has to go to the feminine?

What is meant by "creative disobedience"?

What keeps us from eating of the fruit?

Why is it essential for life that the fruit be eaten?

What happens inwardly when we have eaten of the fruit?

What does it mean to become aware of the good and evil in any given situation?

What is added to life when the Garden of Eden state is changed to one of awareness of opposites?

Why are tensions essential to growth?

How do you experience God's curse when you are put out of the Garden?

What might it mean to be clothed by God after being punished?

What would it mean in specifics for you to step out of some Garden of Eden spot?

What disobedience would be required?

What price would have to be paid?

What would the expulsion from the garden mean inwardly?

Why is it necessary?

Have you ever tried to keep another in a Garden of Eden?

What does such an attempt do to relationship?

What happens to our relationship to ourselves when we try to avoid the expulsion?

Under what condition might one return to the garden?

What would have to be accomplished before the return?

How would the new situation differ from the former?

Summary Questions.

How would you express the central truth you have gathered from this study?

How can one more readily recognize a "Garden of Eden" situation?

What new ways have you discovered to begin to move from the Garden once you recognize you are caught in one?

What, for you, were the newest elements in the concept of God?

Cain And Abel

STUDY IX

Genesis 4:1-17.

I. SYNOPSIS OF THE STORY.

In the story as told in the text chosen for study, Adam and Eve had two sons, Cain and Abel. When they had grown to young manhood, Cain became a tiller of the soil and Abel became a herdsman. One year at the season of the offering up of sacrifices, Cain took his gift from the produce of the soil and Abel took a firstling of his flock as his sacrifice. Abel's offering was accepted by Yahweh, and Cain's was rejected. This made Cain furious, and he did not listen to Yahweh's warning but fell prey to the sin that was "couching at the door." While walking in the field with Abel, Cain's anger at the rejection of his offering overcame him, and he slew his brother.

When Yahweh asked him where Abel was, he replied "Am I my brother's keeper?" At this evasion, Yahweh pronounced severe judgment on the murderer, saying, among other things, that the ground would no longer bear fruit for him and that he must wander about on the face of the earth. Cain, overcome by the nature of his sentence, pleaded with Yahweh saying, "My punishment is greater than I can bear." Yahweh listened to his plea for protection and placed on his forehead a mark that would warn others not to kill him. After a long period of wandering from place to place, Cain settled in the land of Nod and founded a city there.

Sociologically speaking, there are various interpretations of the meaning of this story. It would seem to have arisen in the time when men were beginning to till the soil and thus to reduce the pasture acreage and so cause strife between farmer and herdsman. More important for our purposes though are the psychological implications of the tale. What lies back of this early folktale of the hostile brothers? Here we have the tiller of the soil opposed to the shepherd; the "bad" boy versus the "good" boy; the "rejected" versus the "accepted." In the story as it stands, the accepted was murdered, while the rejected became the cornerstone of a new civilization. What can such a tale have to say to twentieth century individuals?

II. SELECTIONS FOR STUDY.

Cain's Offering Refused — Genesis 4:1-5.

A. Who were Cain and Abel?

    What was the occupation of each?

    What happened to anger Cain?

    Why might Yahweh have rejected Cain's offering?

    Why might he have accepted Abel's?

B. What characteristics do you associate with "shepherd"? With "farmer"?

    With which son do you identify?

    What lies back of your choice?

    What is your emotional response to this episode?

    Where has your inner Cain been angered at the rejection of his gift?

Sin Couching at the Door — Genesis 4:6-8.

A. What action took place in this section of the story?

In your own words, what did Yahweh say to Cain in verses 6 and 7?

(Before discussion read the two additional translations given at the end of the study.)

How did Cain react to "sin couching at his door"?

At what point did the anger become "sin"?

Why did Cain kill Abel?

B. What is anger?

How does it feel to be angry?

How do we repress our anger?

What happens when anger is repressed?

What happens when anger "gets his desire" and takes possession of the individual?

In what specific ways might one work to release repressed anger?

How can one work to avoid being taken over by anger?

How can one work for the transformation of anger so that its energy is positive and flows into life?

(See suggestions at the close of this study.)

Cain Importunes Yahweh — Genesis 4:9-17.

A. What was Cain's first response to Yahweh's questioning?

How was he trying to meet the situation with that response?

What was the punishment meted out to Cain?

75

What kind of punishment was that for a farmer?

How did Cain react to the sentence?

What did such a reaction indicate about Cain?

How did Yahweh respond to Cain's importuning?

What does this say about Yahweh?

How do you understand the mark of Cain?

Why was it set upon him?

B. Who is the Cain within you?

Why is he angry?

How have you experienced a murderous anger?

How does the inner Cain react to punishment?

Why does one need to maintain relationship with Yahweh at a time of condemnation for wrong doing?

Why must we stay related to the Cain within?

How can we work to maintain such relationship?

The rejected, properly related to, can bring in the new. What does this statement mean?

How have you experienced its truth?

Summary Questions and Suggestions.

What was the most difficult part for you to accept in the story?

What was the newest idea you received from working on this material?

What are some of the ways you propose to live the new insight?

Either immediately following the discussion of Genesis 4:6-8 or as a "take home" idea, suggest that the group picture "sin couching at the door." If the pictures are done in the group session, have members comment on the experience. Then suggest that the pictures be taken home for later study. A later write-up about what one sees in the picture can help keep the insights of the session alive.

Two Additional Translations of Genesis 4:8.

1. Why are you distressed
    And why is your face fallen?
    Surely, if you do right,
    There is uplift,
    But if you do not right
    Sin couches at the door;
    Its urge is toward you,
    Yet you can be its master.
    >—The Torah.
    >New Translation, 1967,
    >The Jewish Publication
    >Society of America

2. Yahweh asked Cain, "Why are you angry and downcast? If you are well disposed ought you not to lift your head? But if you are ill disposed, is not sin at the door like a couching beast, hungering for you, which you must master?
    >—The Jerusalem Bible

The Deluge

STUDY X

Genesis 6:5-9:17.

I. GENERAL BACKGROUND.

The myth of a great flood is widespread. There are a number of accounts of floods in various cuneiform documents that have come to light in the archeological discoveries of this century. However, flood myths come not only from this area but from almost every part of the world. The Hebrew version has many points in common with the Babylonian text found on Tablet XI of the Epic of Gilgamesh. The Babylonian text, in turn, has points in common with an earlier Summerian text. The more primitive nature of the Babylonian text indicates that it is older than the story as it is found in Genesis.

II. SYNOPSIS OF THE STORY.

On the face of the earth, things were going steadily from bad to worse until evil was so rampant that Yahweh regretted that he had ever created mankind, and he decided to destroy every living thing. However, he found one just man, Noah, whom he told about the approaching destruction of the world and to whom he gave minute instructions about the building of an ark for protection in the day of devastation.

Though Noah was the laughing stock of his neighbors throughout the years of the building of the ark he continued faithfully with his appointed task until the ark was completed. When the rains finally came, Noah, his wife, his three sons and their wives, and a male and a female of every living creature went into the ark, and the Lord shut them in. The tempestuous rains lasted for a long time, and the face of the earth was completely covered over. After many long weeks, Noah sent out first the raven that did not return, then the dove which returned after its second venture from the ark, with an olive branch in its beak. A week later he sent the dove forth again, and it did not return, so Noah knew that he could now land again on the earth.

As soon as all had come forth from the ark Noah offered a sacrifice to Yahweh. When Yahweh smelled the sweet incense of the sacrifice, he said in his heart that he would not again destroy the earth by flood. Then he made a covenant with Noah and placed a rainbow in the clouds as a reminder to himself to cause no more floods, and this token was to appear in the sky whenever clouds were there.

Again, one finds different approaches to a study of this story. Some take it literally, but they must have a difficult time trying to reconcile the numerous variations within the tale as it now stands in the Bible. Others are interested in the flood stories as literature and in the comparison of different stories from various cultures and geographical areas. This study will deal with the one specific flood tale as found in Genesis. Here we find a vivid cosmic myth told in its own unique form. Behind the story's episodes we shall search out the deeper understandings inherent in all myth.

II. SELECTIONS FOR STUDY.

Yahweh's Reaction to the Wicked Ways of Humans Genesis 6:5-10.

A. In the story, how did Yahweh feel about mankind?

Why was he so grieved?

Who was Noah? In verse 10, how is he contrasted with his neighbors?

Why do you think Noah had found favor with Yahweh?

What is Yahweh's nature as revealed here?

B. What sort of inward state is comparable to the situation described in these verses?

What could make the thoughts of our hearts evil towards God?

How might these evil thoughts express themselves?

What happens inwardly when, for instance, we come face to face with our own violence?

(Stay with these questions until many specifics from the daily scene have been elicited.)

Instructions to Noah — Genesis 6:14-22.

A. What was Noah commanded to do?

What was his attitude to his task?

What was the purpose of the ark?

Who was to go on the ark?

How do you feel about Noah at this point?

B. What are some of your associations to an "ark"?

Why might one need an ark?

What would it mean to build an ark in the face of rising flood waters within?

Why must the ark be ready before the flood is upon us?

What clues might we have that the waters were beginning to rise?

What kind of attitude does it take to build an ark?

Why do the animals have to be taken onto the ark?

How does this fact speak to you?

How might your ark be built?

Noah did all that the Lord commanded. How do you feel about obedience?

What does inward obedience mean?

How would you distinguish between creative and uncreative obedience?

The Days of Flooding — Genesis 7:11-23.

A. How do you picture the days of the flood where no detail is given in the Biblical account?

What would have to be done?

How is life limited at such a time?

(For some delightful pictures of life on the ark see Gaer, "The Lore of the Old Testament," and Graves and Patai, "Hebrew Myth.")

B. How would you describe an inward flood?

What are some of the creative acts that can help preserve life during a period when the unconscious moves towards flooding?

82

What kind of decisions should be left until after the flood?

How might we try to escape the importance and meaning of such an experience?

The Land Redeemed from the Waters — Genesis 8:1-22.

A. Why did Noah send forth a raven? A dove?

What was the sign that the waters were abating?

What was Noah's first act on getting to dry land?

Why did he build an altar?

Why is sacrifice essential at this point?

How does Yahweh respond to the sacrifice?

B. After a time of inward flooding, how might one send forth a raven? A dove?

What is the purpose of such acts?

What happens when we neglect to send out our messenger doves?

God said, "Go forth from the ark," and Noah went. How do we sometimes try to stay in the ark when the time has come to go forth?

In what different ways might we build an altar?

Why is the building of an altar essential at this point in the individual journey?

What things might have to be sacrificed at this new stage of beginning?

The Rainbow Covenant — Genesis 9:8-17.

A. What is the nature of the covenant?

What is its token?

Why does Yahweh put the rainbow in the sky?

B. How might one inwardly experience a similar covenant with the Other?

What are your responses when you see a rainbow?

How might this moment of outer rainbow become a moment of inner covenant?

How would you describe such a moment of inner and outer coming together?

What attitude is necessary for it to bring growth?

Summary Questions and Additional Ways to Work on This Material.

What practical clues did you discover for meeting a time of inward flooding?

What insights came to you about your personal covenant as begun in Study V?

This study is another in which people can readily respond in art materials. After the group response, each to his/her own picture, suggest that each takes the picture home for further study. Additional pictures, models, etc. made at home can continue to open up the deeper meaning of the material.

Ruth And Jonah, Two Telling Tales

STUDY XI

The Books of Ruth and Jonah.

I. BACKGROUND MATERIAL.

The Book of Ruth is an outstanding literary work highly regarded by critics of many eras and many nations. The story was put back into the days of the Judges which fact explains why it follows after the book of Judges. Many modern scholars accept a post-exilic date though there is no agreement among them as to what that date was. The possibilities run anywhere from 550 B.C. to 300 B.C.

The second point of scholarly dispute is as to whether the book is history or fiction. Pfeiffer in his *Introduction to the Old Testament* accepts the book as fiction along with Jonah, Esther, Judith, and Tobit. He gives five reasons for his decision: the significance of the names (Elimelech–My God is King; Mahlon–Sickness; Naomi–Pleasant, delight; Chilion–Coming to an end); the exemplary character of Ruth, Naomi, and Boaz; the picturesque detail of life; the simple, strong, religious faith devoid of dogmatics; and the accidents producing the plot and leading to a happy ending.

The Book of Jonah was written about the middle of the third century B.C. The Psalm of Jonah (2:1-9) was inserted later by the editor of the minor prophets around 200 B.C. Jonah differs from the other books classified as prophecy in that it tells a story about a prophet and does not contain the teachings and oracles of the prophet. There was a prophet Jonah who predicted the conquests of Jereboam II (II Kings 14:25), but whether the author of the story was building his tale around the historical figure or around a purely legendary figure is immaterial to an understanding of his message. To fight for its literal and historic truth is to miss the author's message and to reduce the story to nonsense. Drawing from myth, folktale, and apocryphal sources, the author created this all-too-true tale of the human's struggle against God's all-inclusiveness.

As the stories are short and most of the material in each story will be used in the discussion, they will not be summarized here.

II. SELECTIONS FOR STUDY.

RUTH

The Death of Elimelech in Moab — Ruth 1:1-5.

A. What was the condition in Judah at the outset of the story?

What was the composition of this family?

What was a central characteristic of the religion of Judah as different from the religion of its neighbors?

(Moab descended from Lot who chose to part from Abraham and founded Moab which, like all neighboring countries, worshipped nature gods and goddesses. Fertility rites were part of their religious rituals.)

Factually, why did they choose Moab?

Symbolically, why did they need to go to Moab?

B. What is the nature of an inner famine? How do we experience it?

Psychologically, what was being starved in Judah?

How could Moab supply the need?

What would it mean inwardly to go to Moab?

How does this relate to the general need of our times?

What are some of the areas in which a modern person can suffer an inner famine?

Naomi Chooses to Return to Bethlehem — Ruth 1:6-19.

A. Who were the family members now? (Marriage shifted the family picture; death brought the opposite.)

Why did Naomi decide to return to Bethlehem? (Get beyond the surface reasons to the deeper aspects involved in the situation.)

How did Naomi feel about Ruth's and Orpah's decision to accompany her?

Why did Orpah return to Moab?

What is the significance of Ruth's decision to stay with Naomi?

For what is Ruth choosing?

B. What would Naomi's choice mean inwardly?

Why must the inward Ruth return with Naomi? Give examples of similar moments you have witnessed or experienced.

(Note that the symbolic contrast made here is concerned with the masculine thrust of the spirit in Judah — the push

toward consciousness and the continued hold of the feminine in Moab's worship of an Earth Goddess, soil, vegetation, and fertility rites with its emphasis on the unconscious. Both masculine and feminine principles are essential. Hence, the family had first to move to Moab as the strong patriarchal had of necessity "starved" the feminine. There the situation is changed and the feminine balance of the family now overshadows the masculine. Hence, it is essential that Naomi and Ruth return to Judah to relate the "filled feminine" to the spirit again. The feminine cannot achieve its life in the unconscious alone, nor can the masculine achieve its fullness of being when it starves the feminine. For an excellent article on Ruth by H. Yechezkel Kluger see Spring, 1957. It develops the above point of view through linguistics, early Hebrew history, myth, etc. Likely to be found only in libraries with a large section of Jungian literature.)

Ruth Works in Boaz's Fields — Ruth 1:19-2:23.

A. How did Naomi feel on her return?

In whose fields did Ruth glean?

How did Boaz respond to her?

How did Naomi feel about the way things developed?

B. What kind of inner experience is this?

To this point in the story, how would you describe the inner Boaz?

What would it mean to glean in his fields? To eat with his reapers? To receive extras with his blessing?

Naomi's Plan for Ruth — Ruth 3:1-17.

A. What was Naomi's plan?

    On what social custom did the plan rest?

    How did Ruth respond to the plan?

    How did Boaz respond?

    Why did he send Ruth away before dawn?

    Why the gift to Naomi?

B. You are preparing for a deep spiritual experience. In-wardly, what would it mean to wash? To anoint with oil? To put on special raiment for such an event?

    What would it mean to approach Boaz about marriage?

    Who is the Naomi within?

    Why is it important to stay related to her?

    How is the feminine principle at work in the actual story and in its psychological counterpart?

Boaz Meets with the Next of Kin — Ruth 4:1-10.

A. Who is the first kinsman?

    Why does Boaz have to meet him before the wedding can take place?

    At what point does the first kinsman give up his claim?

B. What is the significance of the meeting place?

    What element in himself is Boaz having to face?

    Why must Boaz face this element before the marriage can take place?

    How have you experienced the first kinsman?

    How can he be brought to the point of giving up his claim?

The Birth of Obed — Ruth 4:11-17.

A. What did the community feel about the marriage of Ruth and Boaz?

What indications were there that this was a special event of great import?

What was the nature of the baby?

What was Naomi's relationship to it?

B. What is the inward meaning of the new birth?

What is necessary if we are to open to a new birth?

JONAH

This is a tale of the Night-Sea Journey — a recurring theme in mythology. It is the death-rebirth motif, an essential part of the individual journey.

Jonah Flees His Task — Jonah 1:1-6.

A. To whom was Jonah sent?

How did the Israelites of that day feel about Nineveh?

How did Jonah run away? Why might he have chosen Joppa?

What happened enroute to Tarshish?

Why was he thrown overboard?

How did the sailors feel about throwing him overboard?

B. How do we often feel about the tyrannical, hated part within?

Why does one fear to show it compassion?

What happens as long as we are in flight against God-given tasks?

Why might we choose a seashore for escape?

Where has your inner Jonah fallen asleep?

What kind of event has helped you back into creative action?

Jonah in the Belly of the Great Fish — Jonah 1:17 and 2:10.

A. What happened to Jonah when he was thrown overboard?

B. How would it feel to be in the belly of a great fish?

What could be a comparable experience?

What are some of the advantages of such a time?

What could be its danger?

Jonah Accepts His Task — Jonah 3:1-10.

A. How did Jonah respond to his task this time?

How did the Ninevites receive his message?

What does this episode say about Yahweh?

B. What is indicated here about the unacceptable parts within? About the nature of the psyche? About the nature of life itself?

Jonah's Response to the Success of His Mission — Jonah 4:1-11.

A. How did Jonah feel about Yahweh's forgiveness of the Ninevites?

How does Yahweh meet Jonah's sulkiness?

What do you make of verses 6-11?

B. How do you feel about Jonah's spirit here? Give illustrations of like responses in your neighbor or in yourself.

What sheltering plant have you been given?

How have you felt when it ceased to protect you?

How have you made its loss more important than personal transformation?

What would working for the conversion of the inner Ninevites mean in specifics for you?

Why is it a God-given task?

Summary Questions.

State in three or four sentences what you hear each story saying.

Which of the two speaks more directly to you as of now?

On what basis did you make your choice?

Songs From The Psalms

STUDY XII

Psalms 126, 19, and 100.

I. INTRODUCTION.

To many people, the Book of Psalms is the best loved and most familiar part of the Old Testament. Revealing a people at worship as it does, it continues to speak to the needs, longings, joys, and frustrations of the human heart. While it is poetry and not prose, as much of the other material used in this course has been, its songs of praise, laments, ritual hymns, confessions, etc. have a deep appeal and can bear much fruit when worked on in the in-depth manner.

As a matter of general interest a few topics of importance in any study of the Psalms will be touched on briefly before turning to the selected texts.

II. THE NATURE OF THE BOOK AS A WHOLE.

Authorship.

In the book as we now have it, some 103 Psalms were attributed to various authors, the others were left anonymous. Of those assigned, seventy were attributed to David. Many of the others were attributed to Asaph and to the sons of Korah whose small hymn books were included in the Psalter. It is not possible to know the author of any specific psalm as it appears today. Some were included because they were attributed to David, otherwise they might not have appeared in the canon.

Structure.

The Book of Psalms is divided into five sections: 1-41; 42-72; 73-89; 90-106; and 107-150. Within these five collections are various earlier groupings such as the Psalms of Korah and those of Asaph mentioned above. Each section ends with a doxology, and the last ends with a doxology to the whole book. While the first divisions come at natural points, the last one between Psalm 106 and 107 seems artificial and was probably made so that the five books of the Law would be balanced by five books of Psalms. It is likely too that the division into 150 Psalms is contrived, for there are times when two Psalms could logically have been combined into one and other places where what has been left as one Psalm might better have been broken into two. To illustrate: the Hebrew Scriptures break Psalm 9 at a different place than both the Greek and the Vulgate do, and as a result the numbering in the Hebrew text is one ahead of the Septuagint and Vulgate versions from Psalm 10 through Psalm 100.

Dates.

It is impossible to give an exact date for most of the Psalms. Earlier scholars tended to lean toward a late dating for a majority of them, but recent archeological discoveries have tended to push to an earlier dating for some Psalms. It is now believed that a number of the Psalms do come from the period of the early monarchy. Others give evidence of being influenced by the prophets, and others are exilic and post-exilic. Pfeiffer believes that the Psalter was attaining canonical status about the middle of the second century B.C. and that it formed the nucleus of the third section of the Old Testament.

Hebrew Poetry.

One fact about Hebrew poetry will help in the appreciation of the Psalms. Parallelism is its chief characteristic, and this characteristic is fortunately not lost in translation. The couplet or the distich is found in a great many of the Psalms. In the couplet the first line is balanced by a second line with the same meaning, with a supplementary meaning, or by the bringing in of an opposite:

> O Lord, how long shall the wicked,
> how long shall the wicked exult?
> —Psalm 94:3

> The heavens are telling the glory of God;
> and the firmament proclaims his handiwork.
> —Psalm 19:1

> If I ascend to heaven thou are there;
> if I make my bed in Sheol, thou are there!
> —Psalm 139:8

Another feature of Hebrew poetry, not conveyed in translation, is the use of the alphabet for binding lines together. The supreme example of this is Psalm 119 where each of the twenty-two sections has eight lines beginning with the same letter of the Hebrew alphabet, and the twenty-two sections cover in turn the twenty-two letters of the alphabet.

Content.

The Psalter contains many different kinds of Psalms, and scholars have classified them in various ways. Most speak from the heart and include the deepest longings and hopes of a people, hence their universal appeal. Both the liturgical and the more personal Psalms include some of life's deepest responses: joy, grief, praise, thanksgiving, sorrow, confession, longing for forgiveness, love, and hate. All the passions of the human being in relation to God, neighbor, and self find their expression in the Book of Psalms.

David and the Psalms.

In the King James version of the Bible upward of 70 Psalms are attributed to David. Even a casual reading of some so attributed reveals the fact that they come from a post-Davidic period and so could not have been composed by David. A majority of scholars today are agreed that while there may be some of David's original work in a few of the early Psalms, it is impossible to distinguish his work from that of others. However, the fact that he has been called the "father of psalmody" did have its origin in very early times and is believed to be rooted in reality. Two pieces of evidence that David was a poet and musician are to be found in other sections of the Old Testament. In the first place the laments over Saul and Jonathan (II Samuel 1:19-27) and over Abner (II Samuel 3:31-34) are believed to be from David. Then in Amos 6:5, the book from the first of the writing prophets, there is a reference to David as a music-maker: "Woe to those - - - who sing idle songs to the sound of the harp and like David invent for themselves instruments of music." (Amos 6:5.)

III. SELECTIONS FOR STUDY

(Almost any one of the 150 Psalms would offer material for inner research and depth dialogue. Three have been chosen as suggestive of what can be done with different types of Psalms.)

PSALM 126

Rejoicing in Relief from Captivity — Psalm 126:1-3.

A. What is the actual captivity mentioned here?

   What was the nature of that captivity?

   What, for many of the Jews, was its chief hardship?

   What is the nature of an outer captivity?

   How might it feel to be a captive?

B. What is the symbol of Zion or Jerusalem?

   What would it mean inwardly to be cut off from the Center?

   What in the collective tends to keep us captive today?

   Where do you feel caught by a collective pressure?

   What does it mean to be inwardly captive to a part of the self?

   What are some of the inward things to which we are captive?

   (It is of major importance to stay with this question until many responses are made, for nothing can be done about being a captive until one recognizes one's captivity. The "captors" include anger, aggression, inertia, envy, neurotic anxiety, will-to-power, etc.)

97

How would it feel to be freed from such captivity?

Write your own psalm of joy for release from some inner tyrant.

Tears and Joy — Psalm 126:4-6.

A. How would you express in your own words the central thought contained in these verses?

How do you respond to them at a feeling level?

B. What are some of the different kinds of tears we shed?

Why is it important to shed tears?

What might it mean to weep "bearing precious seed"?

What is the difference between such weeping and the weeping which bears no precious seed?

How can false weeping be recognized?

Can you share some experience of weeping from which you returned bringing your sheaves?

PSALM 19

(This Psalm refers to no specific outer event and will be treated only at the inner level.)

The Heavens Are Telling the Glory of God — Psalm 19:1-6.

What image strikes you most here?

How does the day "utter speech"?

How does the night sky speak?

What do you feel that the sun means to the poet?

How do you feel its symbolic meaning?

How do you work to stay related to the sun?

What inward attitudes of the poet does this part of the poem reveal?

How does the world of nature speak to you?

Which aspects of the natural world speak most deeply within you?

How might one "escape" into the world of nature?

How, on the other hand, can it be used to "feed" the soul?

The Law of the Lord — Psalm 19:7-11.

What is your first response to the word "law"?

What are some of the attitudes to law today?

How does the poet feel about "the Law of the Lord"?

What phrase strikes you most in the poet's description of the law?

How does it affect you?

How would you interpret the "Law of the Lord" for our day?

How would you distinguish between negative obedience to an outer law and a creative relationship to it?

How do you understand "inner law" or what does a "divine imperative" mean to you?

What is a creative relationship to an inner command?

Cleanse Thou Me from Hidden Faults — Psalm 19:12-14.

Why is it hard to understand our errors?

How would you describe "secret faults"?

How do others often see faults that we think are hidden? (*Give several illustrations to discover the process at work here.*)

By what means have you discovered faults that were at first hidden from you?

How would you define "presumptuous sins"?

How can sin gain "dominion over a person"? (*Again, solicit a variety of illustrations, and work with them to try to discover how sin won the "dominion" and how its hold can begin to be broken.*)

What words and meditations are acceptable in the sight of God?

What might be the nature of the unacceptable in a meditation period?

Wherein, for you, lies the key to acceptability?

(*Note that the unacceptable has to do with attitudes — insincerity, casual, form only, no heart, etc. Anything brought in the sincerity of searching and open to change is acceptable.*)

What are some of the ways you have discovered for dealing with shadow qualities?

What is essential to their healing?

What types of meditation have you found most helpful in this area? (*A deep sharing of experience here can lead to new ideas of time, place, posture, material, order, relation to different symbols, etc., for all those participating in the discussion.*)

PSALM 100

What is your immediate response to this poem?

At what point does it hit you hardest?

What is the nature of "joy"?

How does it differ from "pleasure"?

How can joy become an integral part of worship?

Why are we sometimes "surprised by joy"?

What is your personal relation to joy?

From what roots within the psyche does it spring?

What can block our experience of joy?

How can we work to get through the blocks and so to touch the roots of joy more frequently?

What is the nature of thanksgiving?

What keeps one from having a thankful heart?

What things can keep one from an expression of gratitude?

Why is such an expression essential to fullness of life?

In the human expression of gratitude, how do you respond as giver?

How do you respond as the receiver?

How do many try to evade a genuine expression of gratitude?

What lies back of such an avoidance?

How can we begin to exchange the "Oh, don't mention it," for a warm, accepting "thank you"?

Summary Questions.

A similar theme runs through all three psalms selected for study. How would you express it?

What is the nature of captivity as seen in each Psalm?

How can we become captive to the world of nature? Of law? To the loss of joy and to a thankless heart?

Recognizing some of the pitfalls, how can we avoid them?

How can nature, the inner law, joy, and gratitude, each in turn, help us to break the bonds of captivity and to return to the Center?

Bibliography

Adler, Gerhard	*Studies in Analytical Psychology*
Anderson, Bernhard	*Understanding the Old Testament*
Bewer, Julius	*Literature of the Old Testament*
Buber, Martin	*Pointing the Way*
Buber, Martin	*I and Thou*
Gaer, Joseph	*The Lore of the Old Testament*
Graves, R. and Patai, R.	*Hebrew Myths*
Heidel, Alexander	*The Babylonian Genesis*
Hooke, S. H.	*The Seige Perilous*
Howes, Elizabeth B.	*Intersection and Beyond*
Howes, E. B. and Moon, S.	*The Choicemaker*
James, Fleming	*Personalities of the Old Testament*
Jung, Carl Gustav	*The Structure and Dynamics of the Psyche*
Jung, Carl Gustav	*Two Essays on Analytical Psychology*
Jung, Carl Gustav	*Psychology and Religion: East and West*
Kluger, H. Yechezkel	*Ruth*
Kluger, Rivkah	*Psyche and Bible*
Moon, Sheila	*A Magic Dwells*
Pfeiffer, Robert H.	*Introduction to the Old Testament*
O'Connor, Elizabeth	*Our Many Selves*
Ringgren, Helmer	*Israelite Religion*
Wickes, Frances	*The Inner World of Choice*
Westman, H.	*The Springs of Creativity*